Panorama of Development
Challenges Ahead

About the Editors

Abhijit Guha is Associate Professor at the Department of Anthropology, Vidyasagar University. He has worked on development and displacement and published a number of articles and a book on the subject. Dr.Guha has been teaching in the different areas of social anthropology at Vidyasagar University and taught in West Bengal National University of Juridical Sciences, Kolkata and visiting fellows at the Department of Sociology, Delhi School of Economics and Centre of Advanced Study in Anthropology at Utkal University. E-mail: *abhijitguhavu@rediffmail.com*

Falguni Chakrabarty is Professor at the Department of Anthropology, Vidyasagar University. Apart from his interests in the area of cultural ecology in which he has done his doctoral thesis and published a research monograph and a number of articles, he is currently working on social gerontology and policy oriented research on the comparative study of the problems of the old age persons in the urban and rural areas of West Bengal. Professor Chakrabarty teaches prehistoric archaeology, cultural ecology, social gerontology and Indian civilization and was visiting fellows at the departments of anthropology at Calcutta University and Manipur University. E-mail: *falguni.mita@yahoo.co.in*

Kaushik Bose is Associate Professor and currently Head of the Department of Anthropology, Vidyasagar University. Dr. Bose is a double Ph.D in Anthropology from Punjab and Cambridge University. He is specialized in biological anthropology and has published a number of articles on human growth and nutrition among the tribal populations of eastern India. He has edited a number of books on the different areas of biological anthropology and was a visiting scientist at the Indian Institute of Science, Bangalore and has also taught at the University of Calcutta.
E-mail: *banda@vsnl.net*

Panorama of Development
Challenges Ahead

Edited by

Abhijit Guha
Falguni Chakrabarty
Kaushik Sankar Bose

CONCEPT PUBLISHING COMPANY, PVT., LTD.
NEW DELHI-110059

ISBN-13: 978-93-5125-018-0

First Published 2014

Published and Printed by

Concept
Since 1974

Concept Publishing Company Pvt. Ltd.
A/15-16, Commercial Block, Mohan Garden
New Delhi-110059 (India)
T: 25351460, 25351794, *F*: 091-11-25357109
E: publishing@conceptpub.com, W: www.conceptpub.com
Editorial Office: H-13, Bali Nagar, New Delhi-110 015, India.

Cataloging in Publication Data--*Courtesy:* D.K. Agencies (P) Ltd. <docinfo@dkagencies.com>

Panorama of development : challenges ahead / edited by Abhijit Guha, Falguni Chakrabarty, Kaushik Sankar Bose.
p. cm. -- (Vidyasagar University lecture series in anthropology ; 2)
Contributed articles.
Includes bibliographical references and index.
ISBN 9789351250180

1. Economic development--China. 2. Tribes--India--Madhya Pradesh--Politics and government. 3. Political ecology--India--Madhya Pradesh. 4. Forest degradation--India--Madhya Pradesh. 5. Rural development--India--Madhya Pradesh. I. Guha, Abhijit, 1956- II. Chakrabarty, Falguni. III. Bose, Kaushik, 1962- IV. Series: Vidyasagar University lecture series in anthropology ; 2.

DDC 338.951 23

This lecture series is
dedicated to the memory
of

Professor Ansu Datta

one of the contributors in the series whose untimely demise left a void in the pedagogic arena of the Department of Anthropology, Vidyasagar University

Preface

We are glad to publish the second lecture series of the Department of Anthropology at Vidyasagar University, containing four valuable articles by distinguished scholars which were delivered initially as seminar lectures at our department over the last few years.

The first lecture series entitled *Discourse on Development: Anthropological Dimensions* was published in 2004.

We hope that we would be able to continue with our effort to publish selected lectures delivered by distinguished scholars from various fields who have been visiting our university for the academic benefit of the department.

February 2013
Department of Anthropology
Vidyasagar University

Abhijit Guha
Falguni Chakrabarty
Kaushik Bose

Acknowledgements

We are greatly indebted to the distinguished contributors of this volume who not only responded to our invitation to deliver lectures at our department but they have also sent their lectures in the form of written articles.

We are also grateful to the Vidyasagar University authorities who sanctioned the partial grants from the UGC Unassigned Grants Scheme towards the publication of the book.

We express our gratitude to the Concept Publishing Company, New Delhi for undertaking the task of publishing this book with sincerity and meticulous care.

Last but not the least, we thank our departmental faculties, students, research scholars as well as faculties and students from the other departments of Vidyasagar University who participated in the lectures.

Department of Anthropology
Vidyasagar University
Midnapore
West Bengal
India.

Dr.Abhijit Guha
Associate Professor
Dr.Falguni Chakrabarty
Professor
Dr. Kaushik Bose
Associate Professor and Head.

Contents

Contributors

Ajit Kumar Banerjee is Trustee, *World Wide Fund for Nature* (WWF), India and Senior Forestry specialist in the World Bank. He is a PhD in Forestry from the University of Toronto, Canada and worked as a Forest Officer in the Forest Department of the Govt. of West Bengal. Dr. Banerjee developed and implemented the model of participatory Joint Forest Management (JFM) while working in the Arabari region of the erstwhile Medinipur district of West Bengal. His model of JFM has been accepted by the Govt. of India and different states towards the improvement of forest cover and biodiversity. He travelled and worked in the diverse forest zones of the world including China and wrote a number of technical reports, academic papers and edited books on community forest management.

Ansu Datta was Director of the National Institute of Development Research and Documentation in the University of Botswana. He was also the Professor and Director of the Educational Research Bureau, University of Zambia and was a PhD in the Social Sciences from the University of Leiden, The Netherlands and taught in the Universities of Zambia, Ghana, Delhi, Jadavpur, Vidyasagar, West Berlin and in the Royal Tropical Institute at Amsterdam. Professor Datta has written four books and a number of articles in international journals including *Africa* and was UNESCO specialist in Educational Sociology, School of Education, University of Zambia.

Dilip Mahalanabis is Director, Society for Applied Studies, Kolkata and a Paediatrician and Clinical scientist with M.R.C.P. and F.R.C.P. from Edinburgh. He worked as Secretary to the Scientific Working Group on Management of the Diarrhoeal

Scientific Working Group on Management of the Diarrhoeal Diseases Control Programme, Geneva and also for the Global Diarrhoeal Diseases Control of the *World Health Organization* during 1983-87. Professor Mahalanabis led the team of medical scientists who invented the oral rehydration solution for the control of diarrhoeal diseases in Bangladesh which earned international acclaim and recognition. He taught at the Queen Elizabeth Hospital for Children, London and published a number of articles in *The Lancet*, *European Journal of Clinical Nutrition*, *British Medical Journal* and *Indian Journal of Medical Research*. Dr. Mahalanabis has been awarded an honorary D.Sc. in 2012 by the Vidyasagar University, West Bengal.

René Véron is Professor of Social Geography at the University of Lausanne, Switzerland. Before coming to Lausanne, in July 2010, he worked for eight years at the University of Guelph, Canada, as well as for Trent University, Canada, the Universities of Cambridge and Keele, UK, and the Development Studies Institute at the London School of Economics, UK. He is a Ph.D from the University of Zurich and he has worked in India (West Bengal, Kerala and Madhya Pradesh) for more than ten years. His research involves the study of impacts of globalisation and reform on rural livelihoods; links between state-led development, politics and empowerment of the poor; decentralization and corruption; and institutions in sustainable development, including community-based environmental management. He has published widely on development issues in India, including two books and many articles in international journals, including *Economic and Political Weekly*.

1 Glimpses of China, 1995-2000[1]

Ajit K. Banerjee

Prologue

China is a land of contradictions. But perhaps, all countries can be labeled accordingly. India can also be similarly designated. The difference however is in the nature of contradictions. In India, the most rabid fundamentalist co-exists with the intensely democratic, burkha-clad with the most physically exposed woman in public view, hand driven rickshaws with the satellites. In China, rigid political control co-habit with liberal economy. The village groups look to the village leader or the communist party chief for direction even in daily chores but oblivious of it in individual opportunism.

I was working in China as a forestry consultant (my wife Krishna often accompanied me) during 1995 -2000. My work took me to more than 100 villages along Yangtze river in the provinces of Hebei, Hubei, Sichuan, Hunan and Jianxi . As the work involved peoples' forestry, myself introducing the way the villagers should carry out the participatory micro planning to manage their village forests, it gave us opportunity to see the interior of the villages, its people and leaders, activities and livelihoods at close quarters. We had the chance to meet the village people at their home, in their kitchen, their women and other family members in a relaxed mood. At the same time, the forest officials and often local administrative people of various hierarchic levels would be with me in forest inspections, forestry trainings and discussions, daily lunch and evening food and sometimes in ceremonial welcome and official dinners allowing me to understand their way of life, bureaucratic characteristics, and attitudes. This article records my impressions only of some issues I noticed, selected persons whom I met and heard and a few of the villages that I visited, so the readers can have some idea of the people in general and of the areas I visited, through my eyes. The article is not a researched treatise on China. Except for a few statistics on demography, the data and the stories are what I have heard from the people often about the villages or observed personally.[2]

1. The big China

China is a very large country, three times as big as India, 10 million square kilometers. Its contrasting feature when we compare with India is that China has only 11% of cultivable land compared with 55% of India. It has 41% of its land as pasture and grassland while India has very low percentage of them. 13% of Chinese land is forest, 14% sandy desert, 3% inland water surface and so on. China has a few very large perennial rivers, two well known ones are Yangtze, 6300 kilometers long (Ganges is 2600 Km.) and Huang Ho (the yellow river, 5464 km. long). The country is multi-ethnic; Han is the majority but there are 50 minorities such as Manchus, Koreans, Mongolians, Miaos etc. The language and the script of the Han nationals are the most commonly used and are known as the Chinese (Han) language with a script of Sino-Tibetan family. The scripts consist of pictographs and ideographs, some more than three thousand years old. There are 28 languages among the Chinese ethnic minority.

The Chinese as we all know have a very long history of 3600 years starting with Shang dynasty through Ming to Ching ending in 1911 revolution when San Yet Sen toppled the empire. The Chinese claim to have invented printing, compass, and gunpowder. Chinese-manufactured porcelain, tea and paper during earlier historical times have long been famous throughout the world. Han culture is extremely rich in ancient books and records as well. They had in the past very well known thinkers, scientists, military strategists, writers and artists.

2. Administrative History Starting With Communist Take-Over in 1949 as told by the People

A new government led by the Chinese Communist Party and its leader Mao-Zedong was declared in 1949. A number of revolutionary changes were soon announced and enforced by the new government. The most important of them was distribution of land to the people. The warlords' and landholders' large landholdings were confiscated and the land within the jurisdiction of the village was distributed, to all adult villagers, including men and women, equally. Thus every villager had a piece of agricultural land for cultivation. In most of the areas we worked, the land holding per adult capita was about 0.8 mu (16 mu makes an hectare). The transfer was for use only and excludes ownership.

From 1948-1957, this land and man relationship went on changing by leaps and bounds. First, after the liberation, the farmers who were allocated separate pieces of land to cultivate were encouraged to join mutual aid groups and enjoin their lands to cultivate together (sometimes called production brigade in English) following the pattern evolved in Yenan, a NE province of China liberated in 1946. The problem in 1949 was that the farmers were so poor that they did not have even the draft animal to plough. Some farmers like those of revolutionary Yenan solved the problem by tying themselves together acting as the pull animals and one person steering the plough. Soon these mutual aid groups or production brigades were advised to merge together into collectives and by 1957 many collectives joined to form large communes.

The year 1957 witnessed a first dramatic change in the pattern of development. Instructions from the top of the political hierarchy were received by the villagers to give still more time and energy to the nation to make the nation 'leap forward', to establish backyard steel furnaces to modernize the country and thus disperse the industries. All the village adults including children started making iron ingots in the villages. They established large heating arrangements with makeshift furnaces, brought in iron ores if available near, otherwise iron plates, pans and other cooking utensils at home and used them all for manufacturing home made steel. The furnace was heated with coal or with timber from the forests or with charcoal manufactured in-situ. On the advice of the leaders, community (socialized) kitchens were established in order that the people have more time for nation building activities. In consequence, the labor input on the agriculture land suffered tremendously.

A famine followed the 'leap forward' and backyard manufacturing, and 25-30 million people died of starvation. The leap forward stage was fortunately discontinued and the ingots, the manufacturing equipment of the backyard left to rust and common kitchen was removed in favour of family kitchen of the earlier time. People died but millions of large trees in the forests which supplied fuel in community kitchen and steel furnaces also disappeared. Agricultural production began to increase and the countryside had peace during 1962-69 till the next phase of dramatic change.

During 1969 – 1976, China experienced another big turmoil known as Cultural Revolution. This is well known, but, as revealed during our journey from place to place, and by the responses of bureaucrats and the people to our probing questions in respect of Cultural Revolution, we understood that schools and colleges stopped teaching. Local leadership took decisions, mostly arbitrary, destroying peoples' lives and society. The decisions, sometimes far-fetched, were based on general directions from top hierarchy. As was pointed out by some forester colleagues, we noted later that there is a huge gap, absence of about seven years' of school and college literate people, amongst the present day white colar and intellectual workers, signifying the period of disruption.

The year 1976 turned out to be the end of the Cultural Revolution and beginning of the 'Reform' period in China.

Agricultural communes were discontinued; commune agricultural lands were redistributed to individuals or groups (similar to production brigades of 1950), and contracting land (lease of land for 25 years or more) to individual families was introduced for development. Specialized individual families were selected to carry out special works such as trading, small-scale manufacturing and so on. Agricultural production and per capita income improved by leaps and bounds. The reform in China is still continuing. More economic opportunities to individuals are being provided, now by the state.

In spite of the apparent success of reform, there are plenty of problems and heartbreaks which many people are going through. One of the jokes amongst the Chinese bureaucrats about communism these days is that when the sons do not look after the old parents as they should do, the parents should approach the Communist Guru Karl Marx. And, of course, come back empty handed. They imply that all problems are supposed to be solved by communism but none is ever solved. It is the leaders who control it.

3. My Impressions of China Villages

Let me describe a journey to a village in Hunan Province.

When our car turned from the tar macadam road on to a dirt track leading to the village, I saw the houses, old and some new two storied, in a sea of cotton plants with yellow flowers and some with white cotton blobs. When I reached the village and got down, I saw many old houses having cracks in the mud plaster with an open piece of land in front of them where the family planted some fruit and timber trees. The village road goes by the trees, up and down and sometimes through terraced fields. When going down a steep path, I found a boy of about 16 with a bamboo stick in hand following about 500 Chinese ducks of khaki (beige) color most of which are female but some larger ones which are male and have very beautiful black necks. I asked the boy where he is leading all the ducks to. Through an interpreter, he showed me a pond. It was a sight of so many ducks moving in a deep row, swinging their backs and a single boy controlling them without anxiety. It is a common sight in parts of China, crossing country roads. The boy told us that he has to keep all the ducks in the pond for a few hours and then lead them to a grassland near so the ducks can have their vegetable food. I understood that all these ducks belonged to the village industry and there is a small staff handling them who are all paid by the villagers for their labor. The profit goes to the village for their village committee to decide on its use.

Further on, I met a village lady of about 40 years in a reasonably clean and nice ankle-long dress in the cotton field picking cotton and generally cleaning the cotton stalks. She looked at us and continued working. Left to our winding village path, in many blocks of cotton fields apparently belonging to different families, I saw some women picking cotton and some men were standing near by. I got down the winding path into another smaller path and I found that at the corner of two irrigated paddy fields an old lady is selling vegetables to an old person. This small path took me to a village house. By the side of the house, there was a small and unclean pond where some ladies were washing clothes.

Old village houses in China have a very unique architecture. Whatever materials they are made of, the roofs are pitched, usually of flat tiles, semi-circular pipe tiles, timber shingles, etc. held by very large timber beams with its weights on posts at the house corners and the borders. The posts may be of timber or stones depending on the local availability. The roofs have rafters overhanging the posts and the beams on its borders. Wooden blocks sitting on the posts are the seats of the beams. The blocks called tou-kungs, have arms which bend upwards towards the sky generally only in the corners of small houses or on a number of equidistant places on the eve giving a special Chinese look to the house. The shape and size of the tou-kungs indicate the period of Chinese history to which the architectural form belongs. The new houses on the other hand are more useful but ugly in comparison.

However, brick houses are rapidly replacing old houses in the villages, the money generally coming from the wages of the migrated member of the family or earned by trading. The new houses, sometimes with blue plate glasses, are not so pleasant looking as old houses with tiles. There are three rooms in the ground floor, the central one for the visitors and the bedroom on one side and the living room on the other, kitchen will be on the back of the houses, which are generally painted white. In front of the house is a small piece of land with a few fruit trees which produce condiments or herbs or shrubs . Between the houses or just outside of the cluster of houses, are the agriculture fields and beyond which is the forested areas, or degraded forests or some small rivers flowing over the rocks. Most rivers in China are perennial but some of course, are seasonal. In North China we have often travelled along the riverbed before the rainy season.

The farmer of the house in another village in Hunan called me in his room and we sat in a room. This house had three rooms one of which had all sorts of agricultural products like paddy-rice, some dried vegetables, peanuts, walnuts, dried fish, and some pork hanging by threads from the roof. The room was very untidy with various things strewn in the mud floor. The other room was a bedroom with a large cot almost covering the entire room. On one wall was a small dressing table with a large mirror. On either side of the large room were a portrait of Mao Zedong and a dancing girl perhaps of the new cinema vintage. We were sitting in the center room on a few wooden stools, on the mud floor, the walls decorated with cheap badly drawn and printed portraits of leaders including Teng Sui Ping, Chou en Lai, Chu De, a running horse on a desert, a scene of a waterfall and so on.

The kitchen is quite an important part of the house, with a large fuel-saving oven fed by firewood. In a few houses there is a gas oven and in others we have seen cow dung gas and coal fired ovens. There is no doubt that the use of fuel saving ovens and the dung gas devices are very important strides, comparable to those found in some parts of India. The ovens are big not because there are too many people in the family to be fed but to cook porridge for the pigs. The porridge is made of wild vegetation of all kinds, some left over foods and vegetables and cereals generally millet. This is cooked once in a few days and provided to the pigs, kept just outside the house.

Pigs are very healthy and are kept for meat, for marketing and also for using it for home consumption particularly during spring festivals when the entire family assembles in the parent's home.

All the villages are electrified and the house we were visiting had a black and white television. The electrical wiring is very hastily and shabbily done, thus propped by wooden poles, hanging by the ceiling and the walls. The kitchen attached to the house has got a large oven with two openings, on one of which, was a very large pan with lot of vegetables and cereals in boiling water. I was told that the food is for the pigs, two of which were found in a pigsty almost attached to the toilet. The toilet was squatting type, very unclean, although quite near the house. The landlady was young and well dressed. In came the farmer wearing a mud-splattered gumboot, a straw hat, a gray pant and a red T-shirt. The first thing he did was to roll the shirt up to his neck exposing his tummy and the breast completely. Later I found that this is a very common practice not only in the villages but also sometimes with the officials in the not-too-prosperous township meetings. The landlady explained the purpose of our coming. The farmer offered me a cheap cigarette, which I declined with thanks. He started smoking and answering my various questions.

Not all villages are connected by bus or other conveyance. Walking, cycling and now a few motorcycles are the most common form of conveyance. The loads are carried either on the back or on two sides of a bamboo pole.

Roads in many villages are still often unpaved but the roads connecting the villages are mostly well done and looked after. I have seen very few rivers without bridges along the roads we took from provincial towns to county, to township and village roads. The roads in the villages, unless they are in rocky or sandy terrain, may be quite slippery during the rains. In one of the hilly regions during the rains I had to visit a village through a winding road. It was so slippery that I was absolutely sure that the station wagon will slip off the road and roll down the slope. I therefore almost forced the cars to stop and I preferred walking up the road, which was also a nightmare. Others namely the officials mischievously smiled that I am scared. This is one point that I noticed that Chinese people including the officials are quite habituated to hazards to everyday life including dangerous driving by the drivers, fast driving, jay walking on the roads, where cars are being driven very fast, eating in any roadside restaurants, sometimes with a visibly unclean kitchen and dirty toilets.

Most of the villages in China are developing very fast. Almost 100% of them I visited are electrified, most houses can boast of a black and white TV, sometimes even a fridge and a washing machine. Most of the houses used to be made of stones or else of wood plastered with mud in the hills, say in Sichuan, completely of wood. The recent houses made of bricks are coming up quite fast. In the comparatively mountainous villages, the houses are distant from one to another with some cultivating land or fruit orchards intervening between the two. In the flat areas such as in Jianxi province or part of Eastern Hunan the houses are in one row and close to one another.

A village in China like in any other country has the rich and the poor people except that the difference between them is still not much, although it is increasing fast. The rich people have started building new brick houses, double storied, sometimes with one or two blue colored plate glass windows. The rich farmers have, besides the land like any other farmer, a trading business or have unmarried sons/daughter working in the large town. The farmers sometimes go out to work mainly in construction or other skilled jobs.

The old people, men and women, have to work hard in China villages. Women do all the house work including cleaning the house, washing and drying the cereals, winnowing, crushing cereals, carrying loads from one room to the other, cooking, light agricultural work and so on. The old men on the other hand do the agricultural heavy work including ploughing, harvesting, marketing and the associated works. Once, when I was walking along the aisles of the agricultural fields in one village along with my Chinese friends, an old man stopped me by a sign. He asked my Chinese colleague about me, when he was told that I was from India he came to me and hugged me, asked me my age and on getting the reply told me that "see me, I am old, bent and yet have to do so much of manual work. You are of my age, look younger than me and have a light job". I do not accept that I look younger but I had a feeling that I cannot do the hard work that he was doing.

There is no doubt that the older men and women particularly in the villages look more than their age, their faces quite often lined, body often emaciated, the color pallid and if not involved in land work, have vacant stares. They sometimes live with their grown up children but are generally left out of important discussions and in on-going village activities. I am not sure how they feel, but they are sitting there amidst all the ongoing activities of the home and village but not a part of it. I have seen old people (sometime not very old say 65-70) awaiting death. It is not uncommon to see some blind old men and women, some demented and some schizophrenic.

I believe that when young, the people of China have worked very hard, had been emotionally over-strung for long periods for nation building activities, have gone through much turmoil and have therefore aged faster. The nation building time in the village from 1957-1980, whether for equity or growth, had been a time devastating for the individuals, at the same time this devastating time and such difficult experiences and hard work by the individuals have put the nation ahead and made the villages much more developed, with sufficient food for every family.

My impression of China is that the villages I visited are taking on a new look at a rapid pace. Population is increasing at a moderate pace but many people including women are migrating. If the women conceive by default, they usually abort. A number of village boys are going away for higher technical or general education and once they go away they hardly come home except during the spring festival. They marry in the city and their wives generally cannot lead the village life. Agriculture in the village had made moderate strides from 1947-69 and dramatically from 1977 onwards after reform. Irrigation facilities, use of fertilizers and better seeds were introduced in a very large way by 1969, but after 1977 the productivity increased dramatically. Obviously independent contracted families put in intensive labor to bring about the success. Today the productivity of wheat in China is more than USA although increase of productivity has slowed down in the last few years, but so has happened in USA and Japan. Biotechnology, which promised to revolutionize agricultural production, has not been able to do so.

Major Occupation in Village

The occupation of the villagers varies from village to village but a large part of this is employment, in cultivation. Irrigation is available in most lands where canls from nearby the river have been constructed. Irrigation in many villages particularly in the north China villages is through gravity from a large reservoir built at the highest point of the village, generally the peak of a small hillock or a place similar to it. Water is pumped up to the reservoir at a time when there is less electric consumption, which may be at night. The gravity supply to the agriculture fields is made in the daytime, regulated by a series of well-planned pipelines. I was told that these elaborate systems were laid out by voluntary labor in the fifties and sixties and since maintained by the community. In other places water is also brought in by river lift irrigation, deep and shallow tubewells.

Besides cultivation, people also take to trading, small industry development such as road metal cutting, mineral ore collection, lime manufacture, and finally migrating for part time employment in the towns.

Apart from these small-scale industries sometimes the village undertakes plantations such as that of fruits e.g., persimmon in the north, apples and pears in Central China etc., and tea. I had the chance to see one of the tea terraced plantations. The quality was average and the leader was complaining that his profit from the tea plantation is little and therefore he is not in a position to invest to make it better.

I came across a roadside loading point of persimmon fruits in north China. There were tons and tons of persimmon fruits dumped everywhere and people were loading them in trucks. Persimmon has a very short shelf life and therefore they have to be dispatched quickly. Already some of these became overripe and the owners (the village people) were rejecting them and throwing them on the roads and everywhere making the whole area a quagmire of squashed red blobs of the fruit with a sweet smell. I had a few of the fruits. They looked like overgrown tomato but very soft, juicy and extremely palatable.

Like persimmon, I have seen elsewhere such huge stocks in sites near the villages of walnut, apples and pears in the right season and wondered how is it that we see such sites rarely in India. I believe it is because of the community ownership of fruit trees planted in the village and therefore the operation is not of individual owners with separate piles but all the produce of the village piled high in one place by the community giving it a sight of largeness. This largeness is also visible in respect of vegetable growing land, sometimes in hundreds of acres of rows of polythene covered semicircular (army barrack type of second war vintage) 30-50 meter long, 2-3 meter wide, 1.5 meter high vegetable growing enclosures. The polythene is to keep away the frost and at the same time keep the plant warm. The enclosures with one door opening are irrigated with semi-permanent piped water.

Ba Zi Gou Village

In October of 1996 we visited Ba Zi Gou Village of Gufu Township,

Xingsang County. We were doing forest extension work. A comparatively prosperous family had a brick house where we went to rest and to use their toilet. They also cooked and served the food on the first day. The food was excellent, with tofu (curry for me on request), rice, pork, beef, fish, vegetables and so on.

The daughter-in-law, a very small person running about with an apron over her white blouse and blue jeans, did the cooking. She had her hair covered by a small scarf with flowery design. The mother got all the kudos for the cooking and she never mentioned that is all done by the daughter-in-law. But then the in-law came when the food was almost devoured and started toasting *mao-tai* (very strong wine) with *cambays* (toasts). Although more or less ugly, she made it up with jolly stance, fine behavior and dignified hospitality. During the lunch, a young girl of the middle school in very clean and immaculate jeans and blouse with a blue sweater was trying to practice English with us and failing.

The village extends over 15 km in a highly mountainous region, by the side of a small river. There is a metal road up to the edge of the village and the villagers by voluntary labor were extending the road, which eventually will go to the end of the village. The work was manual, heartbreaking as the rock is hard limestone that needs blasting and manual moving of dislodged rocks off the road. A family of two (a man and a woman) said that they have given voluntary work of 40 man-days each last year. They did not seem to mind as the development only benefits them. The village has 92 families divided into five groups, each having a leader, who represents them in the committee.

We then met the group who would take the afforestation contract. My impression was that the director was excellent in many respects but he pushed what the forestry bureau wanted. Views of the village household's members was not heard. The director accepted our suggestion reluctantly that more discussions should take place with the households before the village committee signs out the contracts with the households. It also became apparent that we were talking with the richest group and the other groups were much poorer. The annual income varies between 2,000-1,0000 Yuan (8 Yuan make one US dollar) per family.

Statistics Talking Villagers but Little Knowledge of Outside

While describing the provincial trips, I had noted that the villager in particular, the village leaders had known the village statistics very well. I would repeat it here to make the point forcibly as I believe it is a very special gift peculiar to China.

In most villages plenty of people could talk on status, statistics and many other intimate affairs of the village. Many of the villagers are good in statistical thinking. However the village leader or the Communist Party leader are excellent in this matter and can go on proudly with the per capita income of the village for the last three years and the present year, the total area of the village, the area of the forest, the area under cultivation, agricultural productivity including the percentage income from year to year for various items. I am not clear if these are correct but these are the official statistics that go to the township then to the counties and finally to the national databank. I give a brief example of a few notes I took from a statement (edited by me) made by a group leader.

In the meeting held with me, the Director, Mr. Wan Xae Ming of the village Yun Feng in Zigui County of Hubei Province told me among other things " Village area is 15360 mu (16mu= 1 ha), 900-1800 m elevation, 214 households, 731 people, village committee of 6 persons, director, deputy director, accountant, security member, youth league member, and a woman member. Of the 15360 mu, 1600 mu is, under cultivation, 8448 mu forests (partly distributed and those in the high parts of the village are still under collective management watched by a village forest guard) and the balance area comes under roads, houses, water body, rocks and stones etc.

Director Gong Wan Xiang of Se Shan Qi village in Zhou Ping Township of Zigui apart from the data of the above type for his village, also said that 'the village per capita income is 312-730 yuan, paddy production 350-500 kg/mu, which gives an income of 1000 yuan per mu."

I quote another example. We visited the village Lu Feng one morning on 10.9.1999 in the township Bai Yun of Lixian County, Hunan Povince. We interviewed three random farmer houses of group 1. The group leader stated (edited by me):

"Per adult cultivable land is low, less than 1 mu but each has some forest and the group has about 2500 mu of forests. The group built a dam in 1980, which supplies water for irrigation. The paddy production is about 6 tons per ha. of hybrid rice. The group has set aside in 1998 about 1000 mu of forests for mountain closure (to rehabilitate a degraded forest). The land belongs to the group but the village committee supervises management. Three people have been engaged to look after the tea plantation each getting 200 yuan per month. Benefit for forest management will be village: group: 3:7."

I am not sure if the data are wrong or right but the people as we see are good in statistics. I have not come across a single villager or a leader in India who could give such comprehensive data about his village.

Although they are so good about village data, few people know of outside world including that of their country. Few people have heard of Calcutta or have traveled outside their states. Even officials can mention only a few things about India except the magistrates with a very grave face who told us that India and China are friends. When I see them I am reminded of our magistrates many of whom have similar routine behaviour patterns.

One of the reasons for the lack of knowledge and paucity of travels outside their village/township is that there used to be a very strict regulation of journey to places outside the township. Secondly, few people had spare money for this luxury of travel for pleasure. If a person has to travel to the provincial capital and stay there for a period of time, he will have to collect a paper from an inhabitant of that locality where he will stay promising that the inhabitant would bear all the expenses of the guest during his stay and if the stay extends, the local committee would have to ensure that a person is going to be employed by some company or other. This was something like a visa that we collect when we visit a foreign country. In the province of Hubei, I was travelling to another city by train. Mr. Chu, my interpreter was with me. A special checker came to us, looked at my passport and the ticket and then the papers of Mr. Chu. The checker was quite dissatisfied with the government identity card and the ticket. It took a long while for Mr. Chus finally to convince the checker that he is a genuine traveller and has been allowed by the government to accompany me. I was told later that he was not carrying a letter from his office that his travel is official.

Every person in China has an identity card and he carries it with him. We also have the voter card these days but I am in no big trouble if I do not have this with me all the time. This regulation of travel has been made in China to stop rural-urban migration, which has clogged most of our cities with slums and unhygienic living of the migrants his regulation has recently been relaxed.

Village Da Chang Chun and Mr. Ben, the Farmer

On 12th March 1996, we visited village Da Chang Chun, Township He Jia Ping in Hubei Province in the morning and then left for the county Cheng Yang. This village named Da Chang Chun is on a plateau, which was reached by climbing on a metal road. The plateau was rectangular, which then climbs again to further mountains still with some snow. The day was warmer and with so much wide space we felt very happy.

We sat in a small room of one household belonging to Mr. Ben. His wife provided us with tea and some nuts.

Mr. Ben was an old man of 60. His face is small and wrinkled with one eye almost closed, but a smiling face. On being asked, he said that the mountain had very large trees but in 1958, the call for backyard steel making saw all the large trees felled by the community (I heard a similar story in the Xingsang County). This was the call by Mao Zedong. In the 1960s, the collectives planted Chinese fir with 80% success. In the 1970s pines, some nuts, lacquer trees, wooden herb trees were planted with about 70% survival rate. Before, the reforms of 1980s, the problem was of management and maintenance. Erosion was heavy especially in 1975, wood used to be stolen by the people for cooking as they were very poor. There was a watchman but he could not watch such a huge area.

In 1980, small pieces of land were given to the households for cultivation. Food problem was solved. By 1983, all lands were distributed. The forests were first distributed partially in 1975 but in 1983 all land including forest-except some about 1000 mu forest, which are too distant and cannot be managed by any, is still with the village.

In spite of this, unified planning enforced all to manage the forest in a specific way. If any person does not do this, the forest or the land reverts to the village.

An old woman said that she has two plots one near her home, and the other up in the hill. My question was if anybody damages her distant plot what would she do, as she cannot watch over it? She said such things used to happen earlier but now everybody has forest and why should they disturb each other? Mr. Chun the local consultant said that affluence of the people has changed all that. It is not due to private forest allotment but more than that the people have the subsistence now, which they did not have earlier.

A Likable Farmer Family

We visited a village in the Chengyang County of Hubei Province. We entered the living room of a villager whose house was on the road we were travelling. The room was small and walls black with smoke from the oven placed in the center of the room. The farmer was a man of 40 with excellent health. He was slim and tall, with a long yellow face and a head full of black hair with large round curls. He was also quite ready to talk but not unnecessarily talkative. He is a farmer with a small piece of land, which is worked by his wife to produce maize and some vegetables. They buy rice which is their staple food. The room we were sitting in had two large pieces of pork meat legs hanging from the room ceiling. There were also baskets full of different medicinal herbs, mushrooms, and corn, all for their own consumption. In an adjacent room, there were big plastic bags full of mushroom. The man of the house explained that he has turned a businessman some five years back. He buys mushrooms locally, dries them in an oven and sells them in two ways. The first is to pack them in small plastic bags of 1 kg and selling them locally. The second is to sell in bulk in Guandzhou. The total quantity he selling is about 2 tons for which he needs a working capital of about 300,000 Yuan, part of which is taken from the bank at 18% interest. He loses sometimes up to 40,000 in a year but usually he makes a net profit of 20-30,000 Yuan. His wife is a pretty, round faced woman, not very particular about her dress, but very efficient and hardworking. She made a delicious lunch for us, with pork, rice and potato chips. While we were taking leave, she said that she is ashamed that she entertained us in a not-too-good house. Her husband said that she is insisting to upgrade the house but if he does so, his working capital will be reduced. I advised his wife that he is right. Let them not block their money in the house. I also said that the beauty of the house lies with the people who live there. The couple with their small daughter, a dog and a cat made a wonderful family in China that I will remember forever.

Farmers throughout the world are a hospitable lot. Perhaps they get a breath of fresh air when the urban people visit them and they welcome them with their best manners and hospitality.

Spring Festival

Spring festival is an occasion of great celebration in China. It is something like the Durga Puja festival in West Bengal, Diwali in the North, and Ganapati festival in the western part of India. In China, sons with their wives, daughters with their spouses, wherever they may be located, would return to their parents' home, for a week every year around February-early March. I had a friend in

Hubei, who would travel by train, bus and then walk to reach his parents house during the spring festival. He was critical and was unhappy that he has to travel such a long distance. Meeting his parents seemed to be a duty rather than pleasure to some. In addition, if the wife had parent's home in a different place also long way from their place of residence, the couple with the child would travel in the spring to the two separate places in alternate years.

The large cities take a very deserted look in the spring festival and so are the shops, establishments and offices. When we used to make our programme for China visit, officials would right away exclude the spring festival dates as being most unsuitable for any official to attend. But so were the X'mas days for the Europeans accompanying us. They would return home invariably before X'mas.

Not only the sons and daughters visit parents in spring festivals, they also have to incur their own expenses of transport, they have to carry a lot of presents from the town to their villages for their parents, brothers, sisters, wives and the spouses, but also for the relatives, friends and acquaintances in the villages. They would also have to carry some money to share the expenses, which his parents would have to undertake. It's a time of great joy for everybody but also expensive for the younger generation. It is interesting how similar customs develop in different but distant centers.

In the festival, every home will have much food, many guests, card playing with stakes, mahjong games for the elderly and playtime for the children with their cousins. Spring festival is actually spread over a week and most of the offices remain non-functional for about 10 days or more.

Every occasion in China is accompanied by bursting of crackers. Even though by 1995 a law was in place against cracker bursting, one can hear this in the villages and in the cities wherever there is an occasion. Very long chains of thin, about 2.5 cm. long small crackers, wrapped in red colored papers are fired and the chain will go on bursting for 3-5 minutes throwing off the exhausted red covered crackers all around the place. Spring festival is a time for much cracker bursting. It may also take place at the marriage, birthdays, festivals and even death in the families.

Marriages

Marriages in China villages are seldom settled. The boy and the girl fall in love and decide to marry, whether in the village or the town. I have talked about village marriages when interviewing people. Generally the boy and the girl are from near families, at best from the next county. They meet either in the village if their homes are near or in the market place or when they temporarily migrate for labor work. They freely mix but unlike the town girls, they do not seem to be physically compromised before marriage. Unlike India, the bride's family is more important and is likely to be financially the gainer. Both families arrange the reception and the house of the newly weds are set up with money received from the invitees and relatives. There is no marriage ritual and a simple registration in the village committee office is all that is required.

One evening in the Zigui county town (Hubei province) restaurant in 1996, we saw a marriage party. They were sitting on many tables and were merry making with the bride and the groom blushing. The two sat welcoming young people. The groom wore a suit and tie while the very thin bride wore a long bright red dress up to her ankle. She wore a coiffure with a few rolls resting on the neck. The coiffeur was sprinkled with golden, red and blue powder. The groom also had powder on his hair. I did not know whether someone had blessed them with the powder. The newly weds were very glad at seeing us. They welcomed us again and again. But when they went away in a car, I saw that the invitees had littered the place with food, paper-napkins, coca-cola bottles etc. They had left the floor really dirty.

In large cities, marriage is similar in pattern but different in its rituals and showier with larger number of guests. The marriage party is held in a restaurant, crackers burst in front of it and guests eat in different tables reserved for the purpose. The newly weds go from table to table and are blessed and wished well. I was invited to attend one such party. There was plenty of wine and food and noise. The marriage was between a driver of a government office and the bride, a technical assistant in the same office. The presents given by the guests may be a strain on their resources. One of my lady friends told me how her husband accepts all invitations and lands her family in serious financial crisis in some months. After all they have to pay about 100 Yuans for each party. The lady was sarcastic and said that the reason her husband accepts invitation to the parties was to drink without restriction, which she does not allow at home. She also said that he is happy indeed when she goes out with me to the villages and he is left alone in their home. She said that he is never alone on such occasions but invites his friends for a beer party and card playing. When I enquired what does he do when she is home in the evenings, she said he is writing last ten years the history of the revolution of China! She did not know when her husband would finish it.

Children and Schools

Education is compulsory for all children, who are found in their school uniform on their way to the school early morning, I have also seen them once a week to go out under the protection of the teacher to do some work outside the school. In one place I saw all members of the school sweeping the dry leaves and dirt in the streets. Perhaps this explains why manual work is not a taboo to the young and middle aged men, women and the old people. The women of the house, even from the comparatively rich homes, are found to carry vegetables or other agriculture products, fodder and fuel wood on their back.

We visited a number of schools and held meetings in them with villagers on Sundays and holidays in different provinces. The schoolrooms are pretty large, with a concrete black board and wooden desks for the school. The walls are covered (sometimes with cobwebs on the ceiling) with large banners, and photographs of national leaders, sometimes with certificates received as prizes.

In one school on a Sunday, I visited the two schools' lady teachers staying in first floor room, which are their living quarters. The primary school was located on a small rise almost at the outskirts of the village I was visiting. The teachers were two young girls of 22/23 years old, one tall and thin with Chinese eyes and the other short, stocky and fair complexion apparently of non-Han origin. They were very friendly and offered me some Chinese tea. They said that the room with two single cots, two chairs and a table with some books in which we were sitting is their only room. They use the toilet located on one side of the school ground. There is no separate bathing arrangement but they use small bowls of water for washing. They cook their own food and told me that they were quite happy. The schoolrooms were clean with very old desks and benches. But the playground was bare, dusty, and merges with the path outside having no boundary wall.

In towns the children are generally very well dressed. Later we saw that in villages also the children were well dressed. Of course in the villages they did not wear the fancy clothes that they wear in towns. But they wear very decent shirts, pants, frocks, caps, etc. In one village, in the rainy season, we had seen children walking in lines through a paddy field towards the school in the evening. We saw everyone wore knee high rubber boots, and raincoats with caps. In winter, I saw the children wearing thick quilted nylon jackets and woolen scarves, caps and mittens. In one of the cities where the hotel was right by the side of a high school I had seen many of the children carrying their own basketball. On the way to the school they would bounce the ball and run to the school. Overall, the children are very well looked after in China.

Hospitals and Clinics

Each village has a clinic of its own. Not very elegant, generally clean (except in one place where it was quite unclean), it is equipped to cater to small emergencies. The doctor is only partly trained to deal with ordinary diseases. They are something like the foot doctors we have read about in books on China. The people, except some old people usually are quite healthy, particularly the children. Similarly, the townships and prefectures have their health care system with better doctors, equipment and act as the referral hospitals of the village primary clinics. In a remote village in Sichuan Province, I saw a very old patient being taken to the city in a chair carried on the back by her near relative.

On 25.10.98, when we returned to the town it was 5.30 PM. We needed to go to the county hospital for a short visit. So we went there straightaway. It was a big hospital, three storied. We had to buy tickets and went inside to see the cardiologist. There were few patients. We saw two very small children also. One of the children had the palm of the hand fixed on a strong plate and there was an intravenous injection attached. His father was holding the pipe and the bottle. The other child probably had something done to his head. There was a very small but neatly done bandage, it was so small that it looked like a band-aid stuck to his head.

It seemed that the hospital used modern equipment. The doctor who wore a very clean white overall checked my blood pressure and said it was fine. He said we should still have an ECG done so we had to buy ticke to for 20 RNB (China's new currency is called RNB, actually Yuan) and had to go to the second floor. A girl was on duty wearing a white overall. There were three more girls dressed in the same way. One of them asked me to lie down on the bed. While taking the ECG the girl complained that since I am hairy (Chinese do not have much hair), the result will not be correct. Anyway she did the ECG and we came downstairs. From a Sony machine the ECG result came out. On the side of the long strip of paper were written the blood pressure and the heartbeat. The doctor downstairs checked my abdomen. He said that we must deposit the price of the medicine. So we deposited 65 RNB. The doctor gave me many kinds of stomach medicine and told me how to take them. On the packets of the medicines, nothing was written in English. There were nice looking capsules, ampoules and packets.

They gave some Gelusil too and I took only the Gelusil.

In the background of this pleasant experience, we also had a bitter taste that came in the evening. There were two doctors; the younger who took my ECG and the other who thought I had a stomach problem. It seemed that the latter did the final diagnosis. I got a phone call and the younger doctor said that he did not agree to the other doctor, who is his senior. He said that I have heart problem and he gave me his phone number in case I have uneasiness at night. I could not make out if this is a sincere doctor doing his duty or trying to prove that his senior is not a good doctor.

My son and his wife (both doctors from UK) came to visit me at Jianxi in 2000 and in one of my village visits I took them to see a clinic in an out of the way township. It was on a dusty road and the clinic was not very clean, the chairs rickety, broken, and a table with old papers untidily kept on them. There were some laboratory diagnostic equipments, some wall charts showing growth of use of preventive medicines and a roster about injections etc. given to each child in the area. My doctor son and his wife talked with the doctor and were moderately satisfied with the attention given to the patients in particular to the children.

Village Protests

I am not speaking of large protests such as that in Tiananmen Square or the ongoing protest and suppression of Fagun Gong. I am speaking of small protests of ordinary individuals or small groups, apparently insignificant which prove that people do retain the fire of protest burning no matter what the form of governance is.

Generally it looks that the village is a peaceful environment with families in a reasonably happy relationship. There is one thing that needs to be said: there is hardly any argument over political differences or violence for it.

However there are protests. Let me now describe the incidents. In one village in the province of Hubei, I, with many forestry, officials had a meeting with the villagers including women as is usual. I asked some questions about aforestation they have carried out, how they are managing to look after the planted area so that it is not grazed, burnt or vandalized, about the degree of participation of various families, particularly in the matter of selection of site, species planted therein etc. I also checked if all have received the wages incentives and bonus due to them. When I was coming down by the sloping road towards a dry riverbed where our car was waiting to take us back, I heard a person running down the road and shouting towards me. I did not understand whether he was saying something to me or somebody else.

He stopped in front of me, a middle aged man in trousers and a torn shirt and a slipper in his feet. He said something in Chinese in a very excited manner which I did not understand. He talked for about 5 minutes without stopping but by this time my Chinese colleagues quickly moved me away to the car. On being asked what the man was saying the village leader explained that he is a mad man. When the car left the place and moved along the dry bed of the river the man still shouting away and the village leader stoping him, his rage became uncontrollable with froth coming out from the side of his mouth. Later on being repeatedly requested by me the interpreter explained to me on a one to one basis that the man was saying that the reports that I have got about payment to participants are mostly wrong. Most of the money according to him was not disbursed. The participants have in fact done the work from their voluntary annual labour input.

I would like to write here about the story of another individual protest in a village. We had been traveling in two station wagons with a number of civil and forest officials to visit a few villages (in the province of Hebei), which were situated on moderately high ridge of Taihang mountains. We are not very far as the crow flies from Beijing but to reach the place we had to come to Sijiajuang, capital of Hebei, which is about 3 hours drive from Beijing. From the state highway our convoy got into a winding and comparatively narrow road, going up the ridge. On the way to the village we travelled about half an hour when the convoy had to stop on a curve. When I looked out, I saw a young man squatting on the center of the road, with his hands folded in humility. The Chief of the Forest official Mr. Yu was also surprised like me, but he came out of the car to enquire about the problem. After he spoke with the man for a few minutes failing to persuade him to get off the road, he came back to chat with a civil official (County Director) who then accompanied Mr. Yu to the man sitting on the road. After a little while, there was an exchange of small slips of paper between the civil official and the man. When he moved away from the center to the side of the road, I found that the man had stumps at the knee and no legs. He had to use two crutches.

Later on through my interpreter I learnt that the man squatting on the road was staging a protest against the village authorities and trying to draw, the attention of the civil official to the fact that the villagers have not kept their promise.

This man was a soldier who had fought in the Vietnam-China war and lost his legs. When he came back to his village having been discharged from the army, it was decided that the villagers would support him for his livelihood so long he does not have any other means of support. The villagers kept their promise for a few years, but a new village leader stopped the allowance. The man came to know a civil official is coming today and hence took this form of protest to draw the attention of the town official to his plight. The official promised by writing that the village henceforth would keep its word.

Later, I found different forms of protest in China. These protests are generally non-violent, occur among small groups and do not generally persist over time.

On one Sunday in Chengdu, capital city of Sichuan, when I was working my computer in Tibet hotel, I received a phone call from my interpreter. He said that I should come in front of the forest office, which was a stone's throw from the hotel to get some new experience. I went over and a saw a large crowd (about a hundred) in front of the closed gates of the forest office and the residential complex. The crowd overflowed from the pavement to the roadway. A few policemen were diverting the cars to the lane on the other side of the road divider. The interpreter, who met me, told me that these men were from the county and township forest office and were protesting to bring attention to the county officials that they have not received their full salary for few months. There was no slogan shouting, a few of them met the officials and dispersed after about an hour. The traffic was, restored to its normal movement.

4. Small-scale Private Enterpreneurship

A Private Planter

In the afternoon, we visited an economic afforestation work by a household in Zing Zia Ping villagein Hubei province. The name of the household head was Mr. Yan Da Zhong.

In this village there were about 150 households but Mr. Zhong was the only one who had taken a large economic plantation. The plantation, that of *Eucomia* (bark is medically useful and fetches good money) is exploitable in 10 years. Mr. Zhong had taken 6 ha on contract from the village. He had made continuous contour terraces, each about 80+ cm wide, 2 meter apart, and planted *Eucomia* at 1 m apart. Forestry Bureau supplied the seedlings. There was no rain or snow in the last three months, an unusual thing, and therefore most of the seedlings (80%), though surviving had top-dried. There was no doubt that Mr. Zhong had done a good job so far except that some of the seedlings may have been somewhat lanky. There was chance of grazing from the local and wild cattle and goat; he therefore had to employ a person watching over his plantation. The number of man-days of labour required for terracing is Yuan 50/ha. All these needed money and the amount of reimbursement for terracing provided by the Government, as an incentive, was insufficient. He therefore had taken a credit of 2000 Yuan from the local Bank, repayable in 3 years and the annual interest was 15%. According to him there was no problem of getting credit, which other villagers contradicted. When I asked him why others were not doing more large-scale planting, he said they were perhaps not so industrious or forward- looking like him. The man seemed to be a very enterprising person. Others in the village had taken small pieces of land for planting timber and firewood. These were done in the slopes and were not therefore so labour intensive as the plantation on the terraces.

A County Private Hotel

We were staying in a private hotel on the river Gufu in Xingsang County during October, 1996. Last time, I occupied a room in a hotel which was facing a video parlor across the narrow road. The private parlor did business up to mid-night at the cost of the sleep of all the hotel residents. This time I therefore chose another hotel.

The problem with this room was the toilet and bathroom. The bathroom on top of it leaked hence the bathtub received continuous drops of water reverberating with a nonmusical monotonous sound when falling on the tub or with a thud on top of your head if you also are taking your bath. I usually took my bath in the evening, as the hot water is available in the evening for a short while. I did not complain because we were no better off in India. I am writing this since I was offered the best suite. At around 10 pm I heard the sound of a Niagra like waterfall emanating from the bathroom. I ran to look for the problem. It was water in torrents coming out of the overfilled cistern. I am proud of being a little mechanic. I removed the cistern cover and then it happened. The water like a yellow stone geyser spurted out and hit the ceiling with the sound of rifle shots. I took a little time, but though totally drenched, finally managed to shut the cistern tap.

5. Tourism and Entertainment

Longmenhe Cave

The Xingsang County Forestry Bureau had built a tourist place attached to one of their state forest parks. The attraction is a cave (Longmenhe cave) about 50 meters long and was full of stalactite and stalagmites, which we visited on 3rd March 1996. Yon have to climb 764 steps to reach the spot. It was a delicate situation for me but I managed to do it. The Chinese way of attracting people is different from others. I have seen such caves in Shenandoah in USA, which were beautiful. The Longmenhe cave is smaller and definitely not as dramatic as that of the US. But the cave has a story of Huang and Chin Dragon kings who have fought here and every shape of stalactite and stalagmite had some significance. For example, in one site the king used to have his seat, in another farmers would assemble the third in were mushrooms which the king would insist on others to eat before he ate them as some of them may be poisonous and so on. The motorable road leading to the cave had, gorgeous scenery and it reminded me of some of the difficult terrains of Bhutan. But the roads were wider and better maintained than in Bhutan.

Dance of a Tribal Lady

In the evening the Vice-Chairman of the Xingsong County Forestry Bureau invited me to see a programme of folk dance. This is a tourist village in Hebei Province; sleepy most of the time except the sound of the train whistles. I do not know why the country will make such a massive investment here of folk dance arrangement. The tariff is 20 yuan (Rs.100 per person), which few locals will pay, perhaps the tourists also will not. It is universally true including in China that most of the 'mass' has lost interest in the old culture. They are interested in the new, in films, in sexy strips, in sports, in nature. The country did not think of them but has set up a folk entertainment place with many buildings designed on the village of Miao tribe of Guizhou (a south-western province of China, east of Tibet). I have read elsewhere that the Miaos at one time migrated in large numbers to Myanmar and Thailand where they introduced shifting cultivation.

Anyway, the dance performance was fairly good, with Mongolian type (short lean and small) tribal men and women in green and white dresses, dancing slow, acrobatic dances. One thing that interested me was that the same person was dancing and playing bamboo flutes simultaneously. This dual activity was a difficult operation and yet the flute was in tune with the complicated acrobatic steps. At the end of dance, a girl dancer came to me and offered me a hollow antelope horn. I did not know what to do but just sipped at its rim and large quantity of very strong liqueur filled my mouth, some of which in fact spilled on my shirt. Everyone enjoyed the scene and I also felt good.

Karaoke Dance

Ninxian county of Hunan Province is of two parts, the old and the new. The new has one very wide road mainly with hair dressing saloons tea houses and karaoke, where people can sing in front of a TV with the song written in bold type, music playing and a lady usually moving about in alluring dress on the TV screen. The county officials took us to a dance hall to entertain us. It was a large wooden hall with a raised platform on all sides. On one side are tables with stools around. On another side are some sitting rooms with couches for 8 persons but no doors. Opposite to this side are small rooms with doors. And the fourth side has the orchestra, karaoke, and a platform for the announcements. Drinks, sunflower seeds, decorated slices of pineapple and the inevitable green tea were served on the tables. Noisy songs by the singers to match television karaoke music and movement drowned all other talk but when a rumba tune out floated, noise filled the air. The dancers moved in, few excellent, mostly novices. Then came the disco and everybody jumped and gyrated. David with a large body, big whiskers and round large face, is a good supple dancer and when he put his hands in the pant pocket, gyrated with the tune in a very relaxed manner, he looked very graceful. All the people danced and I was also invited and to my 'mayo' (means no), they did not agree. The ladies who gave us company were very beautiful, one of them was the most beautiful, thin, tall and elegantly dressed in long dresses, one side of which was cut up beyond the knee to allow easy movement. The dancing-hall owner engaged the girls and pressed them to be especially nice to us. On a lot of persuasion, I finally agreed to dance with the beautiful lady but to my disgust, I trampled the feet of the lady and she graciously said that I am learning fast. Later, I did a number of dances with Miss Heping (interpreter) and Madame He (a forest officer), who guided me. Later in the evening, the girls wanted a photo with a foreigner and then each person took a separate photo for home display.

The old people here are learning their dance with gusto. I see them in the evening doing so in the pavements. There are voluntary teachers and the old disciples are their humble students.

A Buddhist Temple in Nanchang, Capital of Jianxi Province

We walked through a very crowded area at a back street of the hotel where we came across a Buddhist temple. By its side there was a narrow lane just like the lane by the side of Kalighat temple in Calcutta. There were box like shanties from where people were selling wax candles, about 3 to 4 feet long. The candles were colored red or green. They also sold rosary beads, porcelain statues, lockets, cassettes etc. They sold plastic lotuses at the center of which there was an electric bulb. They also sold miniature porcelain pagodas and something else packed in red cellophane paper, which looked like rolls of red ribbon stacked one on top of another. Later on I understood that they were crackers. The crackers are pasted on wide red ribbon. They are taken out and lit at one corner.

To enter the temple it cost us one RNB each. The temple had three enclosures. In the first temple there was a huge sitting Buddha. The room was small, on both sides inside glass cases there were two statues. They had big, scowling eyes like of the "Bhairav". After that there was a small yard. On both sides of the yard there were two big camphor trees. At the center there was a big square box made probably of iron, though it could be made of old brass also. The box was carved beautifully. People had stuck incense sticks inside the box, which was filled probably with ash. The incense sticks here are coloured with a sort of earthy vermilion. They were very fat but they didn't have much fragrance. Probably they were being made mainly with coloured sawdust. The next temple was quite colourful. Inside was depicted the Buddha's life, at the center there was a golden standing Buddha. It was probably as high as four storeys. In front of the Buddha on the floor were spread small, round foam cushions. The people here kneeled down, probably the kow-tow, bending their head and again kneeling erect. There were many statues on all sides at the back wall that had paintings of oceans and mountains and in the midst were placed the statues. Some of them were of the Buddha but others were children, their mothers, sharks, crocodiles etc. It looked very beautiful. Then, there was another yard and a few tall trees and a box where you stick incense sticks, a table round which there were small tools and a few flights of stairs. The next temple was small though on the outside they were painted in vivid colours of flowers and leaves. Inside the Buddha was sitting; beyond it there were a few small rooms inside of which there were more statues of the Buddha. Then there was a platform, which looked like the platform in India in which we have the 'tulsi' tree instead of which there was a statue of a lady with several arms.

All around the temple, on four sides, there were two-storied barrack like small rooms. They were being repaired. Quite a few monks were loitering nearby wearing saffron robes. At one side there was a table and few benches. People eat there nearby where we saw huge pans. One was probably a refrigerator. Here a monk saw me and smiled beautifully and gave me the way. We exited the temple and came on the road.

5. *Mao's Birthplace*

It was a memorable day as we travelled by car about 100 km south

West of Changsha (capital of Hunan Province) to visit the birthplace of Mao-Ze-Dong. In this place, almost all the people have Mao's surname, which means that Mao's clan has lived here for a long time. The place is touristy but of a poor quality as if ordinary folks come to visit it. But most of them and present leaders of China have visited it sometime or the other. We were the only foreign tourists this time. There were many school students in their uniforms, with red scarves and a red flag in front of the two-row formation.

There are four places to see in the area. One is a large standing statue of Mao, of which I took a photograph. This is 10.1 meter high and it was unveiled on 1st October, the Chinese day of liberation, a few years back. The second is his home, very ordinary perhaps of an average farmer of the time, made of mud and husk plaster, tile roofed, the floors are made of mud, some of the six rooms are pebbled, of which one belonged to Mao. The house had a small open place inside by the side of which is a large room where apparently the cattle or the pigs used to be kept. The house has a pond in front by the side of which the relatives of Mao later ran a restaurant. Overall, it is very unimpressive and the maintenance is also not upto the mark. The third thing is a house called Water Drop Cave, where Mao stayed when he came for about twelve days in 1966. There is a small lake here and the mountains on its side have long slopes full of leafy long bamboos, very pleasant to look at. Nobody knew at the time that Mao came here for consultation with some people and left never to return to his home again. In fact the total number of days he was in his birth place after he left for political work first in Changsha (capital of Hunan) is about two years in 1925-27 when he was engaged in political insurrections here and then the twelve days of 1966. The house is one storied, spacious, has an underground chamber in case of bombing. Some of the rooms have sofas for meetings and discussions and a few rooms for resting and working. The third is also a memorial house, quite big with about ten large rooms in a rectangular pattern, has many photographs of the relatives fo Mao and the first and second wives who died, of the statesmen who met Mao, the small gifts given to him, his personal belongings, his cigarette holder, his bedding, books, bookcase, and so on. He seemed to have been a very frugal man who did not waste money on unnecessary things. The memorial was broadcasting his liberation day lecture continuously. The fourth is a Mao clan house where the clan members used to have meetings. This house also has some photos of Mao's ancestors and their memorial articles. On the way back to Changsha, we stopped at the house of Liu Shao Chi in the village Huaniing-lou, not far from Mao's place. His house seemed to be bigger, better furnished but less visited.

6. Governance in China

1. Chinese Command System

China has a tradition of administration by a command system. The system originates with Confucian philosophy (Confucius was born in 551 B.C.), which is still quoted. His teachings advised the people to follow the parents at home and the leaders in the national governance system. Communist China with leaders of the stature of Mao-Tse-Dung, Chou-En-Lai, Chu-Deh etc. strengthened this tradition to perfection. The young generation does not follow the parents but continue to venerate them, religiously return to the forefathers in spring festival and remember them ritually on the days of their death anniversaries. But in the matter of running the nation, the party wanted complete obedience to leaders, which I found again and again while working in the villages of China.

Briefly, the command system is a top-down approach to planning and implementation. It is not with respect to development alone but even pervasive in family relations, community culture, behaviour and customs. I would not like to elaborate it theoretically but provide examples, indicating its main features and impact.

The village institution in China is somewhat different from what we know, for example in India. A village in China has a village committee consisting of a leader and about seven to nine members representing various interest groups. They are mostly selected; only recently elections are being tried in some villages experimentally. There is also a vice-leader responsible to assist the leader besides having a specific functional role. In the committee there is a person who is called the security member to look after village security. There is a woman representing the village women and an accountant to look after earning and expenditure. There is also a member for agriculture and related subjects such as forestry and horticulture. Every village has another leader who is the head of the local communist party. This man may be more powerful than the village leader but not always. The communist members may not be many but they are reckoned more than their weight in number.

Once the policies are passed at the top (the top depends on the nature of policy), the conduit through which it is passed is provincial leaders- county leader- township leader to the village leaders. The authority of the village leader or communist party leader (as the case may be) continues to be substantial, although as earlier stated, this authority is eroding to a certain extent.

Below the village committee is production brigade constituted of the representatives of the families inhabiting the hamlet. Within this brigade, there is again a leader acting as a conduit to pass on to its members the decisions of the village committee (principally its leader). The message generally is passed by the use of hand microphone (now electrically operated) placed somewhere in the village.

2. *Commandism Continued*

I will describe a situation signifying the mindset of the farmers. The mindset is related organically with commandism. One day in 1998, around ten O'clock in the morning, I was walking along a village track trying to locate a person to talk about local afforestation activities under the project I was consulting. I could not see anybody either in the cotton fields or in the houses nearby. The houses were found empty when I knocked at the door or pushed the unlocked doors wide open. I was very disappointed and was telling my interpreter that may be this day is going to be unproductive and that we have to return to our vehicle. Suddenly from nowhere but apparently from the cotton field a man emerged. He was a short man, warmly smiling, very glad that our interpreter started talking with him. She introduced me, and he was all charisma. He agreed that I could go to his house and interview him. We walked along the village track, assuming he is taking us to his house, but at a certain junction he stopped and directed us to go to the path on the left going up a little bit to a house. He however took the right path track after saying a few words to my interpreter. She told me that he said that he does not know what is going on. The only person who can say on their behalf is the village leader, who lives in that house.

As I have said earlier the whole of China even now runs more or less on a command system, although certain amount of decentralization with devolution of power on decision-making is taking place at a very slow pace. One can often read in the major English news paper, China Daily, that experiments are on the way in different part of the country to try election instead of selection of village leaders, county administrators etc.

However, the boss of any office in China, called Director, be it in the capital, township or village committee, is a very powerful man. The Director could, if he so wishes, make the life of his assistants miserable both in terms of pay packet and peace of mind. The assistants therefore keep him always in good humor. At the same time there is far more equality between ranks than what we find in India.

Equality is manifest in a very large number of official human relationships, which we cannot imagine in India. For example even the lowliest like the sweeper can offer cigarettes to his top boss. A middle level person like a driver would always join the lunch and dinner enjoyed by other officials including the chief boss. The lower category officials will easily come into the room of the boss to discuss matters. In China, there are no posts of bearers barring the way of the visitors to the room of the boss.

The rooms of different categories of people are of the same size under same décor. The only difference is that the officials of the higher category have generally one room (not always) to themselves. The tables in front of each official are always empty. There are few files in the almirah. This shows that the clerical works and red tape-ism are comparatively much less than in most countries. This creates of course one problem and that is old data or letters are often unavailable. Now a days, however, computers are much more visible. On the other hand there is no doubt that most of the government offices are over-staffed and are going to be downsized by more than 50%.

Hardly any subordinate official feels threatened in the presence of higher officials. The driver and the first magistrate of the country eat and drink together. The driver of the government car that were used by us in Hubei often made jokes of Mr. Jin, who was the boss from Wuhan travelling with us. Mr. Jin was accepting them very graciously. A driver poking fun at the boss publicly and accepted with good grace is unthinkable in Indian bureaucracy. This making fun of Mr. Jin became a crescendo when the driver and all the technicians were at the dining table 'cambaying' (toasting with bottom-up) at each other.

In spite of the apparent equality however, we could see that there is a very strict hierarchical structure. A leader of the organization is almost like God. He wields all possible powers including annual increments of pay, allotment of houses, allocation of duties, sanctioning of tours and so on.

Let me describe how the Director can reduce his assistants' income. The pay packet of a public servant in an office is rather different from ours. I have heard about it from the forestry colleagues, so what I write below is about the government forest department.

The pay packet comprises more than the pay. One element of

the pay of course is salary an employee gets from the office. This is poor compared to ours. But there are other incomes, which may be a bonus in cash or in kind. These come from the profit of the business that the office runs or from the product that the department produces from its land property. The assistant for example one day might receive 100 apples or 5 bagfuls of rice grown in the nursery land as his share of the bonus. This may come more than once a year. The assistant may sell them or distribute to his friends as he wishes. A colleague told me that the perishables in particular do not bring him any additional income, as he is not able to sell them profitably. The Director himself decides what and how much of bonus he would give to the assistant. Distribution seems to be arbitrary depending on his assessment, which may be very biased according to his personal relationship with the assistants. The assistant therefore has to be overtly friendly to the Director. The assessment of the Director is not so easily contested as most of the Directors if not all are also active party members. It is possible that the additional incomes would equal the regular pay. The Department does not account for these incomes in their books, which means that the GDP reported by the country is an underestimate. I could remember the Chinese Prime Minister once called for revising the public accounting system and among others to include these unaccounted incomes.

Peace of mind of an assistant can be disturbed by the lack of promotions or the pay rises that the Director would decide upon. The words or deeds of the boss are final. Many deputations, tours and part time paying jobs become available to the department. The Director dispenses them to the pleasure and disappointment of different assistants.

In China there is a longstanding tradition that any good idea on institutions, administration, productivity or the like, is tentatively accepted by the top administrators or political hierarchy, is then first experimented upon in a few places, results assessed and if found successful is widely extended with the experiment acting as the demonstration area for others to follow. This method was particularly visible during the Mao era when such large slogans as "Follow X village for Industry or follow Y village way for Agriculture".

In order to show their loyalty to the leadership, the local leaders would immediately follow up the suggested technology or procedure as the case may be, and report in due course the success of their endeavors, no matter what it actually amounted to. I believe there are two reasons why the local leader behaves in this manner. One, they prove that the main leaders in command are right in their perception of the success of the demonstrated area thereby proving their loyalty and thus improve their chances of going up the ladder and second, indicating that they are the true followers of the revolution.

3. *Problems of the Command System*

This command system is like that type of saw, which can cut both ways. If the command is good, the whole system being followed by the command progresses fast. If the command is wrong the system collapses ending up in disaster.

The worst examples of disasters in China are many but I will quote two of them as I have learned from the various village level interviews and the interactions that I had in the course of my work with my colleagues and local officials.

In the 1950s Mao decided, and others followed, that China needs greening, which means large-scale tree plantations should be done mainly in the countryside. The message went out all over China in the name of 4-side planting. People were encouraged to provide voluntary labour to plant trees round their home and village water bodies, round the village, including the roads and along the rivers etc. The villagers planted millions if not billions of trees during this time. Species were selected and supplied by the government. Unfortunately, the stupendous effort to carry out a highly desired activity misfired because of the wrong system of delivery. In a few years, a very large percentage of the planted trees died because the species selection was inappropriate, as it was centrally done not considering the specifics of the local sites and the villagers followed the 'command' without question. Further, the planters did not perceive the effort as an outsiders' project and not their own. They did not look after the seedlings leading to large-scale-mortality.

The second instance, also in the middle of the later part of the 1950s, is the call eluded to earlier for backyard steel making. Mao and the other leaders thought it necessary for the rural people to make a quantum jump from agriculture to the industrial age. They proposed that rural people take on steel making in their backyards. There was a great revolutionary commotion in each village throughout China in response to the call and everybody started making pig iron by whatever means at their disposal and with whichever raw materials were locally available. In many places the raw material for making pig iron was the kitchen pots and pans and people cut the trees to use as fuel for heating. From village to village during my interview I was told that the largest valuable trees of the their local mountain forest were cut down at this time leading to deforestation followed by erosion. In continuation of this order, the central directive to the people was to discontinue the private kitchens, create community kitchen and supply free meals to the people so that everybody is available for the great leap forward. Private kitchens were stopped. The common kitchen led to overeating and wastage. The local leaders tried to prove that the common kitchen is a good idea and is sustainable, quoted inflated local cereal and vegetable production figures to the township leaders who in their turn to the county leaders and finally to the party headquarters and the central leaders. This was an ecstatic time where all basked in the glory based on wrong figures of production in terms of quality and quantity. In fact, the people did not give attention to agriculture and the productivity fell drastically rather than going up. Within a short while, there was food shortage leading to one of the biggest man-made famine in China around 1960s. There are lots of differences in the number of deaths reported by various agencies but it is no less than 25 million people.

It is obvious when one discusses the matter with the local leaders and the people that the problem of this system of governance namely, command system is still not very clear to the majority. In my interface with leaders at various levels, I was often surprised when they did not realize that their system is one of 'command'. They insisted that their governance was very participatory. Millions of days of voluntary labor by the people, great marches towards the production sites of people carrying banners, shouting revolutionary slogans, all these taken together, looked to them to be a manifestation of participation. Generally the leaders are blind to the fact that participation is freedom to decide. In a command system, decision is taken elsewhere and the work is only carried out by the multitude without questioning the justification of the decision.

4. *Kowtow to Leaders Showing Signs of Retreating*

Only recently, even in my 5-year time frame, I saw the situation changing with colleagues justifying Madame Chiang and even Lin Biao. Hush-hush things in the country are slowly but perceptively disappearing. The best example of this change was what I heard in September of 2000. My friends in De'an County of Jianxi Province took me to look at the burial grounds of Hua Yeo Beng, one of China's Presidents who died in 1990. The site chosen is wonderful, a lonely large area in front of Poyong lake. It encompasses a reasonably large round hill with the burial monument at its flat peak. You reach it by climbing 72 (8 and multiples of 8 are symbolically good luck and praiseworthy) easy steps, with a group of steps alternating with a few meters of flat area from the next group. You are not therefore fatigued. The burial slab is irregularly quadrangular, not high but gracefully rising up with cypress trees surrounding it. The stone is of granite and there is a black stone at the base on which some of his achievements during (1915 to 1990) are written in Chinese. The Chinese Girl Guide was explaining to a group of visitors that Mr. Yeo Beng did not bow his head to

Deng Tsiao Ping. I got the full story from my interpreter. Mr. Yeo was supported by Deng and Chou En Lai to become the party secretary and later on President as well. During his presidency, the Tianan'man square student uprising took place. Government rudely suppressed it on the advice of Li Peng (adopted son of Chou, later the Premier of China) and by Deng himself. Yeo Beng opposed it and refused to cooperate with the party line. He was banished from the Party and was placed under house arrest. He was reported to have died under mysterious circumstances, either committed suicide or by poisoning. During his burial ceremony, Deng did not want to come. The people of China wanted him to come and he came. Thousands of mourners insisted that he bow to the coffin, which he finally did at least once. This story is now being told and therefore Deng also is not sacrosanct. Truth is coming out and is being discussed.

Further stories we heard are about Deng and Zao Zemin in Younxi County in Jianxi in 2000. It appears Deng's sons became millionaires during his lifetime. So too did Zao Zemin's. One of the sons of Deng went to America with millions of dollars. Another son is disabled and is the trustee of one of the important trusts in China.

Zemin is becoming unpopular in China, being a person trying to be on the lime light all the time. He travels all over the world and is seen in TV with his mechanical smile. He is not worth much. On the other hand, Premier Zu who is hardly seen in TV and seldom travels outside China is a darling of the country. He is considered to be an economist and a practical man trying to fix many wrongs in China. It seems for Zu, sincerity and humility pay.

5. Nationalism

Another name of commandism is Nationalism although achieved through a different route. Nationalism is aplenty in China, ingrained in the thought process and the government encourages it. China can make no mistake when there are some problems between nations for example, China-India war. Most people believe their government-sponsored newspaper verbatim. For example, China Daily, the most circulated newspaper, talks mainly of the achievements, seldom of problems, protests and failures. Unlike us, the ordinary people and the highly educated would never criticize their country. I am very surprised at this as I had the wrong understanding that communism promoted internationalism. The manifestation of nationalism was at its zenith during the US bombing of Bosnia. An American bomb fell on the Chinese Embassy, by design or mistake, and some casualty occurred. The Americans said that it was due to a mistake in the map and the Chinese said it was deliberate to teach the Chinese a lesson for their lukewarm support of the war effort. Be that as it may, the government promoted a national frenzy and the civil society responded to it adequately. For the next week, a weeping father walking down the ladder of the plane grieving for his daughter killed in the bombing was repeatedly shown on the TV. Then some locals attacked Americans and foreigners in Chinese cities. One day in a county in Jianxi, I was going to a restaurant for lunch with my Chinese colleagues along the pavement lined with small stores. A tomato missile just missed my head and my colleagues immediately surrounded me and took me away from the place hurriedly. I saw a very tall and robust angry young Chinese in the shop looking at me with red eyes. I was apologetically told later that the man mistook me for an American man. But nobody thought that this promotion of nationalism was in vulgar taste.

6. Discipline

The word 'Discipline' has often been misinterpreted, but I use it in the sense of doing one's committed duty. They do, but in view of overstaffing of the public offices and the public sector industries, per capita administrative productivity is low. It is a very common thing to see staff whiling away their time in the offices, except one or two who would be busy. But the infrastructure has improved tremendously. Most offices are equipped with the latest models of computer. Chinese language software is loaded in all of them and people at all levels thus can understand the message. Most offices even in small townships have a conference room for providing extension of technical know-how and also semi-political messages. The villages have the mike system announcing to the people messages and meetings of the day. In spite of per capita low productivity, the infrastructure has made good the deficiency. An economist can argue that mechanization without reducing staff is faulty economics.

The people in most places in China are busy becoming rich and they have no time to look for less pollution, less smoking, less drinking and so on. I feel that this breakneck movement towards economic prosperity is a reaction to the belt tightening accepted by the whole nation trying to succeed in communism in the earlier decades. It seems that communism, by making bureaucrats economically suffer (pay being small) for the nation as a whole have made them more thirsty for the good consumer things of life and hence are the excessive drinking, smoking etc., by some.

Another thing that should be noted while discussing the change relates to an observation by a village leader. He said that the households no longer follow his advice. They go on their own. They come to him only when there is a chance of getting some benefits from some source. This to me is a significant statement as it shows that the whole leadership system of yesteryear is now falling apart. This is the first social indication of liberalization. It is not privatization of property, which is democracy. It is the feeling of the individual that he thinks for himself and has the right to express himself. Voting is much talked of but is a totally false proof of expression of individuals. The expression should be on everything that affects him. If he does not get a chance to do so as it happens in most so called democratic countries of India type except during periodic elections, then it is pointless liberalization. I only hope this does not happen in China. In China this is the time to introduce decentralized micro-planning, i.e. provide everybody an incentive to be involved in all the issues that matter to him. A serious society will make this endeavour. Or else such societies will end up a highly stratified society where revolution will break out. I am not against revolution in states where the system stinks. Where there is a chance to go through decentralization to the end which revolution tries to attain, do it when there is time. And China perhaps still has the time and India does not have it.

7. Habits and Mores

1. Unclean Personal Habits

Some women and men, more the latter, show unclean personal habits. In one village the chief of the township (like our Block Development Officer) and the village leader and his wife were continually spitting in the mud floor and were squashing it with their shoe. In the best hotels, the people leave the fish and meat bones on the table by the side of the plates. Of course the tabletops have tablecloth and that too covered by a disposable fine plastic sheet. Even in township hotels (one star) the toilets are really bad. In the villages, each house has a toilet but they are somewhat neglected. This is however better than in India where the whole countryside is a gigantic toilet. The river side in China is not so clean because of for human dung. It is because they pay little attention to civic beauty. Yet, they have so much beautiful crafts, colourful folk music and dances, pantomimes, magic shows, delicate paintings, and lovely old architecture. I think they have a compartmental mind. When they think of beauty, they do so in their art pieces, which are not reflected in their everyday life, which is a separate compartment. I can say the Bengalis are lucky that way. Every aspect of our daily chores has some beauty stamped on it. Think of the paintings in front of the village houses, on the floor during Lakshmi puja, thousands of pandals made in the Durga puja, saris of women who have not still changed their attire in spite of so many provocations like crowded buses etc. Perhaps, there is another reason in China for neglect of beauty in everyday life. It appears the pictorials Chinese scripts in small, medium and large sizes has replaced other drawings and paintings.

2. *About Tips, Theft etc.*

Workers in the hotels, restaurants etc., except in the recently established private hotels, do not accept tips. In fact, the hotel girls did not take fruits or other food such as nuts, biscuit packs if we offered. We got these eatables from the forest department in plenty for munching after dinner.

Theft is little in the villages and small towns. People usually say that there is little theft in the villages. At least I have not lost anything in the villages (anytime in China). We have reached villages where every householder is away either to the field or to the market and the house door is just closed without any lock. We have gone in and called out to see if anybody is home. But I am not sure that it is true everywhere. At least in two villages, I have seen ferocious dogs chained in front of the house making it obligatory to take a detour while nearing those houses. These dogs are not pets but guarding dogs. The new houses have window grills. Presence of a security member in the administrative village also points, perhaps to prevent disputes between families and so on rather than to theft of house property. Timber theft from the village forest is not rare and illegal hunting needs police control. In the township hotels, there is always a caution about theft of personal belongings, which they advise you to guard against. These notices seem to be precautionary although in real terms, petty theft is really uncommon.

But cycle theft is a very common occurrence. One could see once in a while a young man looking desperately for his cycle in the stand with cycle lock key in his hand. This loss does not evoke any sympathy to the onlookers who rather cursorily note it with disdain or take it as a joke with a smile. The old cycle market in the country is huge. You would see few new cycles, not because the user cannot afford it but to ensure that the cycle does not attract the attention of a thief. A colleague told me that some of them intentionally keep their cycles dirty to avoid theft. Dacoity is occasional especially in large towns but they are negligible compared to what we face even in small towns. Murder is rare.

3. *Copying Habit*

There is another interesting thing in many provinces perhaps this is true of humankind, the habit of copying others. In China, the present sense of beauty in architecture is use of ceramic tiles on the outer wall and then painting them with gray cement. Blue plate glass is another fashion found almost in any new house being built. There might be however one reason for this blue glass uniformity namely the standard of technical advance. Later in 2000, I saw more and more of plate glasses of other colours; apparently the appropriate technology for other colours has been introduced.

4. *Drinking and Smoking*

Drinking is also a very common feature in the province. I have seen very few inebriated people on the village roads. I would record one incident of drinking. It was around 10 p.m. at Guangyuan city in Sichuan. We have finished our supper around 8.30 p.m., but I was called down to meet a lady social scientist from a charitable institution in England (she knows Chinese language and with relish told-me how useless my work in participatory forestry would be as I do not know Chinese) doing participatory work and staying in the hotel. When I went there, I was sorry to see that two Chinese foresters working with her were totally drunk and were behaving in a rowdy manner. They were throwing glass tumblers at each other and we, including the lady scientist just saved our heads.

Almost in every grocery and multi merchandise shop in the

villages, on the roadside, townships, there is the sight of hundreds of beer bottle waiting to be picked up by the suppliers. Restaurants of all kinds sport Mao-tai wines of several brands. Also very common is smoking. I am surprised to see that a number of people smoke, much more than in India. Everybody has a packet and is offering to the other. The cost varies from 1 Yuan to 10 Yuans. The average cigarette packet is 3 Yuan (about 40 cents) which is quite high. Mrs. Song, my interpreter, told me that her husband smokes about 30 cigarettes a day and that costs about 100 yuans. According to her this is good money in China where average income is about 500 yuans for an office assistant. Drinking and smoking are most common in lunches and dinners.

5. *Lunches and Dinners*

Many times I had been invited in the village to have lunch, sometimes we would have the family interview in a home with the cooking of our lunch in progress. The lunch served in Sichuan and Hunan is excellent at least to my taste. The food is spicy and the dishes are of vegetables plucked from their own fields and also of wild vegetation. The vegetables are of different types of lettuce, squash, pumpkins, gourds, peanuts, cabbages, cauliflower, eggplants; soya bean curds in two or three forms and some local fish or chicken would always be included amongst the menu. In the richer households, there will be pork brought down from their stock and deliciously cooked with some vegetable and thick sauce curry. The rice would be generally cooked and served at the end of the lunch. Beer in the summer and some local liquor would be provided and the whole group with the family members excepting the women would be sitting round the table enjoying the meal with gusto and taking easily an hour and a half. Cheap cigarettes would be liberally distributed and smoked by almost every body. The dishes don't arrive at the same time but come one by one but fast, hot, spicy and delicious.

Let me describe the features of official lunches step by step.

We first troop in a restaurant at exactly one p.m., One p.m. for lunch and six p.m. for dinner are almost religiously followed (no matter what the other compulsions are at the time) by the officials, which used to be a joke among the consultants. We take our position in a round table in a large cubicle with the important host at the center, the main guest at his left facing the entrance door and the next important guest to his right and other guests as near to the host as possible taking precedence over others. All the plates that will come one by one as the lunch is on, will first arrive near the guest and the host and then only will the others help themselves from the plate. When the fish comes, generally a large steamed fish with the mouth a little open will be placed in front of the guest. Then the guest will accept two mao-tai toasts. Passing on the plate from one to the other is possible as the table is equipped with a lazy boy at the center. The people round the table with their chopsticks pick up any food from the plates without any systematic sequence, unlike the Indians. The last plates of rice (steamed) bread or dumplings, are served in small ceramic bowls.

The food is excellent but not so spicy in Hubei or Hebei as we will enjoy in Hunan or Sichuan. The Chinese have the knack of making simple food complex and good. For example a simple thing as duck egg is kept for a long time in tea and when boiled is a dirty green egg with a totally black yoke and delicious too. Pork is the main meat but sometimes beef, chicken, fish, and frog legs are added. The number of courses (plates with different food) may run to twenty. These include the special fresh water fish of the Yangtze. The vegetables are plenty mainly green leaves, lettuces of different varieties, cabbage and of roots such as potato, radishes, onions and others. Mao Tai is a strong liquor (55-60% alcohol) and is gulped without soda or water.

But the real fun of the dinner is the toasting and overdrinking of Mao-tai. The younger people take beer in summer. Every county boasts of their special Mao-tai. The toast is an excuse to do bottom-up (*cambay*) gulping of strong wine. The toasting every time is mostly for a single person and seldom for the group. I also saw the other day a magistrate toasting to the German visitors four continuously consecutive toasts and each one with a different toast. The first one is that he is so happy that the German has come. Second that he hopes that he will enjoy his stay. The third is to thank him for working so hard and so on. The main topic discussed in the later part of the lunch or the dinner is manoeuvers why one or the other should have another toast, and the other person trying to avoid the toast. But finally he yields and they have toast. These verbal encounters, one person trying to have a *cambay* (bottom-up) and the other trying to avoid it take place continuously as a mock fight. It seems everybody learns these methods and the encounters may be interesting as it appears to me from their face, which takes a very peaceful but sometimes prolonged mock argument with many others taking one side or the other in arguing the case of one party or the other. I do not understand the language but when translated they seem to be nice but fake dialogue. But what I wanted to say is that they drink a lot in the lunch and the dinners in particular but I have, except on two occasions, one described of student behaviour earlier, hardly seen anybody drunk.

To add flavour to these toasts, some new ideas were introduced by a German consultant, whose company I enjoyed. Whenever possible we would work together. He loved his drinks and he was most entertaining during lunch and dinner hosted by the Chinese. He introduced a number of new features in the '*cambay*'. When somebody offers a toast with *cambay* (bottom-up), you can request the person for a reprieve with '*bambay*', which means that let us have half of the glass. You have to of course entreat and get the consent of *bambay* from the person offering the toast. I was found entreating all the time, as too many *cambays* would start a splitting headache. The one person who started the idea but never entreated for *bambay* is the inventor. He was my mentor and would compensate my failure when a person asking for a toast will not relent with my entreaty. For example, to reciprocate to accept toasting I would say that we consultants work together and my friend consultant would take over my part as well in wine toasting while I participate in the beer. Another idea was that after a *cambay*, you have to show that not a single drop of the wine remains in the glass. If it does, the failed person has to re-do a cambay as a punishment. Many failed in the job for enjoying a second *cambay*.

My description of the lunch and drinking should not be extended to the everyday lunch in a family or of an office goer. During lunchtime, you will see many people going about their chore with a bowl of rice and some vegetables and occasionally eating out of it with their chopsticks. I find that this eating habit, while walking or working, is an obsession with many or is it a tradition! This is a typical lunchtime scene in middle class or poor locality and quite different from the scene we see in our country.

7. Sports

One thing that I always think is how China has done so well in sports when there was not a single instance where I have seen any children playing any game in the villages in the provinces we have visited. There were hardly any playgrounds. In the cities, you only see them playing snooker on the billiard tables on the pavements. Only one time, in the province of Hunan, we saw from our hotel window a basketball ground on the yard of the next building. It was a very cold morning, but we found series of groups of boys apparently at prefixed times were coming in cycles to practice under the direction of a coach.

One explanation is that the excellence in sports has been brought about by a top-down and elitist approach. The administrators decided to get prizes for the prestige of the country. Some promising young boys and girls are picked up who are then trained to become the heroes. This is unlike America where many play, swim and some of them come out successful. In America, the driving force is the money that will come to the winner in sport once he has done well. Here it is the sweat according to somebody's idea and prestige. None of these driving forces is commendable but in America you have the option to play and enjoy. Here it is a task to be performed well and the pleasure is a by-product.

One of the jokes made by the Chinese to me was in respect of Indian standard of sports. At the time of my stay the Olympics was going on and the Chinese were piling up gold medals. Different people would ask me how India was faring. I would say that we believe unlike others in sporting spirit and not in medals.

8. Women

1. General

In earlier times, women in China, were subservient to men. The families were patriarchal; the head of the family, sometimes consisting of 4 or more generations, was the oldest man of the clan and on his death the elder or the most worthy son took the charge. In the villages, usually the married brothers separated, the brothers headed the families, although they used the same meagre assets that their father possessed. The women did not inherit and went on serving the husband and later the son.

During the Chinese revolution, many young women in China joined it. The women often accompanied their husbands and fiancées and suffered untold miseries including martyrdom for the cause of the revolution. Many leaders had their wives with them and some of them were leaders on their own merits. We know of Madame Chiang, wife of Mao, later considered as renegade, as one of them.

Among the peasantry, the women were very active in household works as also in the agricultural work. The emancipation of women actually took place with the success of the revolution. During the enthusiastic economic development of the countryside that followed the revolutionary triumph in 1948, the women like the men joined the huge labour brigades to provide voluntary work in building dams, roads, state houses, tree planting, soil conserving, river training and related works. During the Cultural Revolution of late 1960s and early 1970s, the women students took an unusually active part. 'Wild Swans' the autobiography by Jung Chang testifies to this fact.

The women in Xingshan, a small county (Hubei Province) for example, are definitely more advanced than our women in small districts. I saw a number of women running three wheelers; some are driving buses. The people quite often talk about the mistakes made by Mao but one thing they acknowledge is that he emancipated women. There were not many signs of Mao but when we went to the villages, we saw Mao's posters in the main room of the farmers, homes (they call this room as guest room).

In 1995-2000, the women were all over the place. In addition to serving the usual professions that we see the ladies in India today involved in, namely in office administration, teaching, hawking, sweeping, in big business etc. you would see them in moderately large numbers in China also as taxi drivers, bus drivers, field foresters, field geologists, policemen, and in any other profession. The women are locally very mobile. We saw few simple things that however point to the progress of women. We would just mention one such. This was in a small township hotel in 1996. We were not been able to plug on our laptop. There was only one plug point in this room and our TV was plugged on there. When we told the management of the hotel, they sent a lady. Last night water was dripping on to our bathroom from the bathroom on top. The cistern was also spraying water. The problems could not be rectified. They only brought us a bucket of water. We changed the room in the morning. Now we saw it was the same lady who came earlier. She brought an extension chord with a plug point, which was a very expensive and foreign made. Soon we had the TV and the computer working together.

Unlike many parts of India, most women may it be in villages, towns or cities, in particular the younger generation, use cycles without inhibition. Thus on any day, you would meet them on foot, on cycle, in bus, train, plane and wherever you look. In the villages, they are hawking, drying cereals, ploughing, sowing, planting, seeding, reaping, and carrying cattle feed or busy in household chores. In marriages, the men have to pay to the women's family not the other way round. In cities in particular, the women manage the household finance and the men often are under the control of the wife, not an uncommon thing in India.

In spite of apparent equality however, there are indications that the women still are, though not as much as in India, subservient to men. Discrimination is evident when we heard of ongoing girl infanticides still in some places and the silent women in the meetings in villages I attended. The women would attend but would, with a few exceptions, need a lot of coaxing to take part in the deliberation. Generally, they would suckle their babies or would be talking to each other or be engaged in weaving, stitching etc. This is almost a scene similar to those found in many parts of India. Another evidence of discrimination is the presence of some men who are silent but become vocal when they meet a girl. That is what I see in two of my Chinese colleagues here. Both use a bantering tone when they are vocal to women, every word having double meaning creating mirth in all men and also a hollow laugh from the lady. As soon as she is gone, they are again silent, somber and sad and absorbed in their own unknown thoughts. This would be considered harassment in many developed countries.

2. About Some Women We Met

In 1998, in the province of Hunan, I was traveling in a team of my Chinese colleague, the lady Deputy Director of the project in the county. The third member of the party is my interpreter and the driver. We have a car with us, which will take us to different places for about 14 days.

The interpreter lady is short, with thin features, thin face, long hair, very well dressed and is quite a personality. She can be quite tough while arguing and has leadership qualities. She is elegant in her bearing with modern pattern of behaviour, like and dislike. She apparently comes from a comparatively well-off family and lives with her parents. She is not married. When not in office, she spends quite a bit of her time in restaurants, good films, picnics and so on. She likes to drink a glass of beer when offered and is a firm believer in equality for women. In no time, she started a flirtation with the driver and obviously both were looking for opportunities to be alone. The other lady is just the opposite. She is trained in forestry in Nanjing University, which shows that she is a good student. She did so in 1992 and has already reached the grade of Vice Director of the project. She is also short but has a square face, short hair and is a very soft-spoken pleasant person. She says how she controls the finance of the family, does not have a child as yet and is quite straightforward when talking about her in-laws who apparently try to influence their lives. She is a typical worldly women found throughout the world, pleasant, not flirtatious but helpful, is somewhat rustic, and non-interfering. When she talks on any subject, she gets excited with a lot of hand movement, which makes her look quite impressive and serious. The driver, as they usually are in China, is ambitious, behaves like a king when in his car, and tries to upstage all the passengers. He is married, talks about his child but was temporarily carrying on with the interpreter.

My wife Krishna records an incident about a woman in Hubei. A very young girl came to us and started a conversation in English. She spoke haltingly but her accent was totally American. She asked whether the town was beautiful or not. She said that she was a teacher in a school in the town, previously she used teach Junior High and now she taught Middle High. When we asked where she had studied she said that she had studied at Ethan for three years in the Teachers Training School. They had two American, one English and a Scottish teacher at the training school. The school she teaches now has 1000 students. There are about 120 teachers. The school has two terms and the tuition fee for each term is 700 RNB. That meant the annual tuition fee was 1400 RNB. She said, the next day was "Sports Day" and asked us if we would be able to attend the "sports". She said she had to attend a meeting in the evening. After the meeting she would come again and meet us at the hotel.

Let me talk about women of Hunan and Sichuan in general a little. I quote from my diary. "I can distinguish generally four types. There must be many others. One is the grandmother in the city and the villages. The ones in cities are short, humble, shabbily dressed mostly lazing on the roadside, or taking care of the grandchildren, playing cards, doing simple exercises or taking dancing lessons in the park with the husband in the evening. The ones in the village are short, with small feet, going about all the time like a worker bee, moving a basket, sweeping the floor, cooking something, winnowing, collecting mustard seeds, like our women do in the villages. The second type is the middle-aged leader in the villages, government offices, friendship stores, malls and plazas. They are bored, non co-operative to customers, reading books or newspapers, weaving wool or stitching. Those in the private companies are more active and receptive to customer needs. The third category is the blue-collar workers, in the factories, bus drivers, and such occupations. They are very energetic and most enterprising. The fourth category is the younger ones. They are a mix of types, not for their age and clean and colorful turnout but for their totally different outlook from what I have seen elsewhere. They are as if awake from a sound rest (together with strength) and having done so are moving at a tremendous speed to reach some new destinies. They have not only taken over the leadership at home in respect of controlling the money but are also outside on the run to generate more income. Many of them after their office work manage small businesses and are aggressive to make it successful.

In Chaotian County, province of Jianxi, we were taken to a restaurant for supper. Midway, a woman of about 30 came and introduced herself as the owner. She was tall, with round Chinese face, dressed in a black long dress with black shoes, and a husky voice (I think done intentionally). She told me that I am the first foreigner in her shop and therefore she would like to offer a toast. She said a lot of good words in that hoarse voice and then offered a beer (*phizo*) *cambay*. And then went on doing so with all the other six on the table, smiling a sweet smile, unperturbed with all those glasses of beer enriching her blood with alcohol. After she has finished our room, she went to the next table in another room and did the same with the same husky voice, a sweet smile and this time with Chinese liquor. She said that she does another job and this business is not for money alone but it also gives her a lot of satisfaction. I think this is a true statement as many Chinese women of this category are really enjoying life of this type for the first time and have made this their true goal, the goal of money and external connection of flamboyance, good dress, excessive make-up, continuous talking, and alluring people and making money. I am not complaining but I think they are going the way of the Thai girls, lack of depth with a lot of apparent freedom. This is somewhat misplaced progress unlike that of the west or even of India where the spirited girls are for NGO, environment, forestry, anti-dam, anti-relocation, for tribals and so on. I did not meet a single girl mentioning this type of problems with any gusto.

I record another example of an enterprising woman. We had to hire a taxi, as the number of officials were too many to load into the Pajero car. The taxi lady came to me and offered to take me in her taxi so that her taxi can take a foreigner for the first time. This is a ruse, as she knows that I will pay better money. When I did not agree, she said that she has also a barbershop and she will like to wash my hair at 10 Yuan. Short of any physical contact, she did used all her charm, cajoling, entreating, and making a sad face, flirting, praising, etc. on the director to get that business. My Chinese friend, the director of the county agreed that he would do so when they reach the barbershop. When we did, the director said that the shop is shabby and he will not have the wash after all. Then the lady used all her ruses all the time saying 'chima' 'chima' meaning please, please, but the gentleman did not agree. Having agreed and seeing that the lady was on the verge of tears not so much for the slight loss of business but having failed to take us in, I agreed to get the hair cut.

The Chinese women are confident, in good health, although still discriminated in the long run. The cases of girl infanticide are its evidence. But the women are coming up quickly, only I think by a wrong route; a route of selfish mental development without utilizing its choice of other options, options of knowledge, protest, equality to men.

3. Prostitutes

China seems to have come of capitalist stage truly at least in the sense of women offering their physical services. I noticed a sad thing on 13th March, 1996 when we were returning by car from a township to the county headquarter Changyang. In two places at least on the road, well-dressed girls signed the car to stop. These were near hotels in out of the way places. I was told that they attract the drivers and offer them hotel food and night stay, of course at a price. In other words, it is broad daylight prostitution promoted by hotel owners. Earlier I had the impression that prostitution has appeared in an uncontrollable form in the coastal cities but this has now made deep inroads.

While in a park in a pleasant lighted evening in a county in Jianxi, I saw a girl to our immediate right reading a book in the park lighting, which was sufficient. There were two young boys sitting on the same place but left of us. One of them went up to her and proposed something and she declined. I thought he took her to be a prostitute. At night in the hotel I was awaken three times by a girl and a boy proposing something I did not understand.

In the last fortnight in May 1998 in Nanchang capital of Jianxi Province, girls approached for prostitution in two places. First was in a small country hotel. Around 10.30 p.m. somebody called me on the phone and I thought it may be some forestry colleague checking if everything is fine with me. But she was speaking in Chinese and I thought she must be some hotel staff. I said I speak English, and she started giggling and then another girl came on the phone and somehow managed to say that she is Chinese. Anyway then it dawned on me that they were offering night service. I said sorry. Next day it was worse. After I checked in around 3.00 pm, a call came through with giggling and I again said sorry. After about 30 minutes, I heard a knock on the door, which I opened and a young girl entered into my room. This is how every waitress comes in here to do the room and brings hot water but she was a prostitute. Not yet a professional from her dress and looks. She was young, in a half shirt and a black half pant. When I folded my hands like they do here to be modest and said that I am sorry, she did not know what to do, also said sorry and walked out. But they are persistent. Half and hour later another call came in and I did not pick up.

Interesting however is the fact that by 1990 when the government took a very severe attitude to prostitution, this problem in hotels had altogether stopped.

4. *Leader Woman*

I came across a woman leader in a village in Jianxi. She was about 25 years old and belonged to a poor family; I interviewed her not in respect of forestry but more about her life and the opportunities that facilitated her to become the leader. Her father was a leader about a decade back but fell from grace. Her father tried to educate her and after she finished school she was to be sent out to college. She passed the inevitable entry examination and was selected for college education, a very important feat. Her father was accumulating a little bit of money for her education and her stay in a hostel away from the village. At this time a quarrel arose between two families, theirs and a neighbour, which turned somewhat violent. One of the members of the neighbour's family got injured badly and was treated in a city hospital. The village community decided that the girl's family would have to pay for the treatment of the injured person. In consequence, the fund accumulated for her education was all gone and her dream to become college educated disappeared forever.

She continued to stay in the village and worked like any other village women. She is however very sober and continued to keep up with her education by reading books, newspapers and talking about the things she read with other women and sometimes with men and somehow the whole village decided that she should be the village leader. She was a novice in the job, and shy with foreigners, often dictated to by the men in the village, but I found she had a determination, which I hoped she would use for promoting village development. This was a rainy season and the undulating pathways in the village were literally in quagmire. I was going from house to house interviewing people and she came out with me putting on a gumboot. I found that the families I was interviewing were particularly friendly to her.

She is not the only one. I have come across some young girls, who were smart and ready to take up more responsible occupations than doing daily chores of village life. One thing that was not clear to me was the fact that in many villages, the wife had gone away alone to a distant city such as Shanghai for years together for work. Their husbands on questioning were vague in explaining they were still a part of the family sharing the family expenses and returning once in a while to their home.

The women, particularly in cities and even in small townships, are quite carefree about exposing most of their body except their breasts. In daytime in summer, many of them would go about in short pants and T-shirts. In the offices, they would be in full pants and shirts or in narrow skirts and tights. The old women in the villages still go about in blue Mao suits but the younger women would put on pants, shirts or thin acrylic garments. It may seem to be unlikely but even during a short interval between 1990 and 2000, the women's dress and style have made great strides. I took this change as a part of progressive emancipation of women.

5. A Waitress

The waitresses of the breakfast room came to talk with me to polish their English. This is done by many in the streets who would run to me to say 'hallo' or 'good morning' and then run away. While talking with them, I came to know that one is from Hainan islands studying hotel management. She has been allocated for two months in this 5-star Sun Shine Hotel as an apprentice to learn hotel management. She said that she is unhappy as she was not circulated in departments but for the whole two months is allowed to remove food plates and guiding the customers to the seat in the restaurant section. She also said she gets 150 RMB a month, which is really low. The other girl was a regular employee. She said that she wanted to change jobs for many reasons that I did not explore. On inquiry she said that they are two sisters and one brother. The brother worked in Nanjing airport factory, the sister in the school, both very meritorious. She thought that she was the stupid one. She disappeared for two days and on the third day told me that she went to look for jobs. She got two, one as a secretary and the other as telephone operator but could not take up any as she fell asleep and could not get up on time. I asked whether she had an alarm clock, she said, 'yes', but failed to hear it when it rang. She also said that she had a headache because she was looking for jobs in the daytime. The other day she also said about headache because the meeting room was stuffy. This is a thing I found with many Chinese middle class. They are more comfort loving than their counterparts in India.

6. *Temporary Emigrant Woman in Shanghai*

I was sitting in a house belonging to an ordinary peasant. This house is made of wood, covered with tiles and had two large rooms. There were many large wooden stools which were offered to us for during sitting on, the interview for which I came to his house. The farmer was not well dressed; he looked dark compared to a Chinese. He looked very sad but was quite ready to talk about his life, his lands of a few mu of cultivation and about his wealth. Wealth as I could see in his rooms included a TV, quite inconsistent with his other properties such as a bed, chairs, tables, stools, agricultural implements. When I was looking at the TV, he told me that this had been brought from Shanghai, where his wife worked. He showed me a picture of a young lady well dressed standing in front of a gate of a large factory of Shanghai. This lady did not really fit the shabby house and emaciated person with whom I was talking. The farmer told me that his wife works for about 11 months in

Shanghai in the factory producing linen goods for export. She comes back for 3 weeks every year. The husband could not tell me why he sometimes did not visit his wife in Shanghai. Later on, I found that in many villages, the ladies rather than the men were migrants. I was not also sure but my interpreter told me that some of them were also sex workers.

9.Individual Portraits

1. *Professor Zhang's Life*

At Guangyuan, (May, '98) Professor Zhang narrated his life history. His English was just understandable, having most of the alphabets so softly spoken with the abundance of c's and s's. The professor was tall by Chinese standards. He was thin, flat with more width than thickness, long face, slit eyes, flat nose and the mouth with jutting teeth, the center one visibly missing. He looks more aged than his age (about 60) but was agile, wiled to walk very fast (much faster than me), chimbed mountains like a goat in his rubber shoes and spoke with substance. He told many stories from ancient times. He was politically mature with analytical mind and a benevolent philosophy like a Buddhist (although he did not believe in it). He quoted what my mother told me once that always look down to see how many are poor and not to look up to see how many are rich, to decide on one's life style and to assess apparent disappointment and failures. He was also romantic and told me about a poem written by a famous poet of ancient times (of Tang dynasty). He also recited it in Chinese after the story was narrated (he had a pleasant voice unlike most Chinese who have a sharp and thin voice). The story is that of a lonely man who missed his beloved who was alone in a distant place for a long time. The man, sitting in a wild garden on a moonlit night by the side of a gargling rivulet said that he was alone with his shadow and the distant moon as his only company. But then his beloved also had the company of the same moon, however distant the Moon is. So they had a common bond, the bond of the Moon.

The story of the professor was that he was born around 1940 and was the son of a landlord. His father however understood the history and gradually gravitated to revolution. In the liberation of 1949, they lost their land, money and in 1956-59 all other possessions. They were therefore declassed. The professor in the meantime had finished school, college and university education in forestry and had started teaching. However, during his career, he got a chance to work in the embassy in Norway and was also involved in export-import business and got chances to stay in Norway and became rich there. He was also in the USA for a year or so, did not explain how as a professor he got these chances. Anyway, he was back and loved to teach. He then retired but taught on a voluntary basis. During the 'Cultural Revolution', he was thrown out of the college and sent to his village where he planted peanuts, paddy and other things and was involved in doing all kinds of menial chores. He did not approve of this method but was not really vociferous in his condemnation of the Cultural Revolution.

The professor said that Mao was all right at the beginning but degenerated by 1960s and his role was poor subsequently as he accepted the wrong advice. He criticized the present young generation saying that they did not think of the country but of themselves, only about more money, more consumption. They have forgotten the Chinese struggle, its revolutionary history. He thought that being an old country China had the disadvantages of large population and baggage of historical mistakes. They needed rectification before new things could come. He said, "See America". They could build from nothing as per their own design.

Professor was getting 400-Yuan up to 2 years before last, which was then increased to 800 Yuan per month. He used to get a pension of 55%. That is sufficient for his family of two, he and his wife. His two sons and two daughters were on their own.

10.Epilogue

I am not going to write about what happened in China after 2000.

We have read about them in newspapers, published papers and books. We have read about its joining WTO, having second highest foreign exchange reserve, developed countries investing billions of dollars in Chinese economy, high rate of growth, improving economic life of their people, more economic and social liberalization and at the same time continued wrap on the political freedom of the people.

In this small chapter I will write about two things about which I sketchily recorded in my diary. They are environment and effect of human institutions on individual character. My diary notes on the topics are miniscule indeed but I have taken the names of such important topics, as I did not get any other appropriate name.

When I was younger I used to think naively that one of the reasons the socialist countries could never economically compete with democratic countries as former overspends on protecting environment including pollution from industrial business. This idea was destroyed first when Chernobyl disaster happened and later during my China visits. It appeared to me that China gave little attention to increasing pollution from various industrial and service sectors in the last two decades when China started industrializing at a very fast pace. We saw people covering their nose with kerchief while going about their business in Beijing and Guanzhou (earlier Canton). During the same and earlier periods, a lot of high forests and animal life were destroyed with many flora and fauna (example Giant Panda) in the endangered list. The corrective actions China took for forest habitat deterioration included large-scale afforestation (one of the largest in area in the world) and establishment of protection forests of different categories, but these could not restore the lost biodiversity. In spite of afforestation, deforestation of high forests is still going on albeit at a lesser rate.

In respect of environmental pollution, I like to pick up a small paragraph I wrote for a village in the province of Hebei. In the village, I was told that I would be able to buy locally manufactured gold. When I went to the village (not for buying as it would be illegal) I was pleasantly surprised that almost every family in the village is collecting gold ore from the local hill and extracting gold by mercury using a few small locally made machines. The ore was crushed, sieved, washed with water and then treated with mercury, mix churned, and the amalgam passed over a copper plate with coating of mercury. The amalgam of gold and mercury sticks to it and other materials pass through and are disgorged as effluent in a nearby small stream. The amalgam was then evaporated to separate mercury from gold. The process seemed to suggest that all the mercury is recovered. In fact is it was not. The plate did not trap part of the amalgam and thus mercury got into the stream. Secondly, while evaporating, part of the mercury was mixed with the air. Thus one can imagine the state of the local air and the chemical contents of the water in the stream, which the people in the lower reaches would use.

I would accept if somebody says that my samples were too small to come to any conclusion about China's record on environmental protection. I saw plenty of damaged forests and heard about deforestation many times from the people. I would like to say that that record of China in the matter of ecological preservation is nothing special to be proud of. It is as good or as bad as in India.

I assumed that as Chinese people had after liberation gone through cooperative and communal living, the people in general would be less individualistic and particularly less selfish in their behaviour to fellow beings. My conclusion, based on a number of observations some of which have been noted in the earlier narratives, was that that there is some difference but not so significant compared to average people like us grown under competitive capitalistic society. For example, many Chinese people would often be naïve and would really not understand what is official corruption. Some of them, particularly in the villages, would believe the leaders to be beyond any wrongdoing. The labour brigades of several families sometimes of the same clan or the same hamlet would take up many activities together without any friction between individuals.

In many cases in villages, the close neighbours would help each other in ploughing, building own houses and even in more arduous jobs. Such neighbourly help is, however, not unknown in Indian villages as well. I would however end my comments with a real life incident about an individual. I think he makes the difference.

In November 2000, in Nixian County in Hunan Province during a banquet, a high official of the administration was present. After a few courteous words, and a few *cambays*, he did not talk to me more. The gentleman was pleasant and I noticed that he was very earnestly talking with the rest of the group. He talked more while others were mainly listening. I remembered our older days when the seniors in the hierarchy talked and we listened. Yesterday, my interpreter told me on her own what he was talking. I realized that I was seeing a very great man and in fact I missed a classical story of the man's ethical commitment. I have no chance to congratulate him now and express my best wishes for him.

The interpreter said that the discussion started in respect of the recent government declaration to combat corruption, which was raising its very ugly head in the country. This man, being a high official took upon him the directive with all earnestness. He first looked into the inside matters of a state owned factory. He was surprised to see that the director was corrupt, but he was very popular. He was providing all sorts of facilities including some presentation and money, which did not appear in the budget, and were given to a few according to his wish. On further enquiry and exploration, the gentleman found that the entire staff of the factory was involved in corruption in collusion with the director. He thus proceeded against the men. Then to his surprise he found that his wife although not directly related to the factory was indirectly associated with the corruption as well. He did not stop, but went to prosecute all including the wife. The wife is in jail now and would be there for a total period of 5 years. The husband had also returned the money to the authorities in installment, which his wife misappropriated. He said that he would take back his wife, as she will be reformed.

My sampling of more than a billion people of China was really small but yet at least I met one person of a very high standard. I am sure there would be more. But so are some of them in India.

Note

1. This travelog was written by the persistent requests of Abhijit Guha who first insisted me to deliver a lecture on my experiences in China while we were on a tour to some villages near Medinipur town in connection with an action oriented research project. I delivered the lecture at the Department of Anthropology, Vidyasagar University on 22 September 2003 but was a little hesitant to write it in the form of a chapter for the Lecture Series, since I am not an anthropologist by training. Finally, however I had to write being fully aware of my limitations. The readers, particularly the professional anthropologists may not consider it as a typical ethnography of China, but I am sure they will find many interesting factual materials on the social life in rural China for further study.
2. Here, I would like to make it clear that China like many developing countries, is constantly on the move towards changing policies, strategies, governance, attitudes, and so on. Even during the short period from 1995 to 2000, I observed dramatic changes in some places although in my narrative I restricted myself to the period of my visit. Anthropologists may prefer to call it the 'ethnographic present'.

2 A Tale of Tribals, Traders and Tubers

The Political Ecology of Forest Degradation in Madhya Pradesh

René Véron

1. Introduction

I feel very honoured to have been given the opportunity to give a well attended lecture at Vidyasagar University in front of such a highly respected audience of anthropologists, economists and other scholars. I am also very grateful to have the chance to publish my lecture in this format and, indeed, to reformulate and improve some of my arguments. Thanks to the comments from the audience.

Being aware that most social scientists at Vidyasagar University are more familiar than me with "tales of tribals and traders", or of rural development and forest management initiatives in India, I am trying to make an original contribution here by viewing one such tale from Madhya Pradesh in the context of globalisation and by interpreting it from the theoretical perspective of political ecology. This tale, or case study, centres on forest change and, more specifically, on *safed musli* (*Chlorophytum borivilianum*) – the tuber mentioned in the title and a valuable medicinal plant and non-timber forest product (NTFP). Taking a political ecology approach encouraged me to consider the material, ecological properties of this tuber in the analysis of socioeconomic and environmental change and spatial restructuring that have occurred in the recent past.

This case study was conducted within the context of a broader collaborative research project.[1] In section two, I will describe this interdisciplinary project's overall research questions, applied key concepts such as "globalisation" and "sustainable livelihoods", as well as the methodology of the study. Section three summarises concepts and theses of political ecology, the theoretical perspective applied here, as they appear relevant for this case study. In section four, I briefly describe some forest dynamics in Madhya Pradesh and in section five, link these environmental transformations to wider political-economic changes that are related to globalisation, economic liberalisation and political decentralisation. In section six, the implications of resulting socio-environmental processes are examined for the sustainability of poor people's livelihoods, in particular those of *adivasi* populations. The paper concludes in section seven with some remarks on the empirical study of globalisation and the suitability of the theoretical framework of political ecology.

2. Context : The project "Globalisation and the Poor"

As mentioned above, the case study of this paper has been conducted as part of the larger research project "Globalisation and the Poor", which included three economists from JNU, a retired high-ranking civil servant from Delhi, as well as two political scientists, an anthropologist and a human geographer from the University of Guelph. Furthermore, six Indian and Canadian graduate students as well as further research assistants and interns were involved in the collection of data. Such a large number of researchers with diverse disciplinary backgrounds required substantial coordination, which has in part been ensured through the participatory formulation of overall research questions, the identification and definition of a few theoretical key concepts, and a common but flexible methodology for quantitative and qualitative village studies.

Right from the start of the project, however, it was realised that individual researchers cannot and should not be straitjacketed by any rigid theoretical approach and methodological framework. Soon we found that it also would be very difficult to establish generalised causal links between globalisation/liberalisation and livelihoods. Therefore, we decided to complement our macro- and micro-level data collection with original individual case studies cutting across spatial scales. The case studies were on soybean agriculture, labour migration, privatisation of education, corporate marketing through self-help groups, and forest change including the NTFP sector. These case studies were chosen because of their importance for livelihoods and their particular relation to liberalisation and globalisation.

1. Overall Research Questions

One of our project rationales was to see how globalisation and reform policies have manifested themselves in a comparatively "backward" and "peripheral" state of India. There is a dearth of sound *empirical* studies on the relationship between globalisation and livelihood change, particularly in areas that are at first sight not very much linked to a global economy and polity. Madhya Pradesh seemed particularly under-researched. Many people in New Delhi suggested that globalisation should rather be studied in more "advanced" states such as Punjab or Andhra Pradesh. However, we soon found that economic and cultural forms of globalisation have found their way to remote areas in Madhya Pradesh too, albeit in sometimes indirect, complex and ambiguous ways.

The project's overall research question was a very basic one: How have globalisation and reforms affected rural livelihoods of poor households in Madhya Pradesh? Making my influence as a geographer I felt, the project from its beginning has been sensitive to spatial variation. The objective was to conduct studies in three different major agro-ecological zones. We also attempted to consider distance from transportation lines and commercial or political-administrative centres as an independent variable, which however proved methodologically problematic so that we had to drop that idea.

To approach our overall research question, we first attempted to identify globalisation and reform processes in Madhya Pradesh that are relevant to poor and marginalised men and women, including *adivasis*. This first step is important since globalisation processes most visible to an outsider, such as India's boom in the information technology sector, for instance, may not be that relevant for a tribal peasant in Madhya Pradesh. Secondly, the project endeavoured to ascertain what economic activities have gained or lost in importance after the implementation of reform policies since 1991. Linked to this, we asked the question of spatial shifts of economic activities that are gaining or loosing in importance. Thirdly, the project attempted to examine the implications of the identified socioeconomic changes for different social groups among the poor. Thus, apart from spatial variation, we were also sensitive to social variations acknowledging that "the poor" cannot be analysed as a uniform category. Indeed, we assumed that implications for livelihoods and vulnerabilities of the poor may vary between men and women, different ethnic and occupational groups, different regions, etc.

2. *Conceptualising Globalisation*

To define and conceptualise "globalisation" in a cross-cultural, interdisciplinary research team proved to be a formidable challenge. Different perspectives and understandings coexisted between us. While our Indian economists tended to view globalisation as the opening up of international and domestic markets brought about by economic liberalisation and reform policies (particularly since the New Economic Policy of 1991), the Canadian anthropologist, for instance, was more interested in social and cultural transformations towards some form of modernity that are facilitated by communication, mass media and markets. The political scientists, by contrast, were keen to understand the changing capacities of the state and sub-state units in the liberalisation era. What we had in common, however, was a willingness not to exclude any of these views about and aspects of globalisation but to integrate them as far as possible highlighting their interconnections. We were also aware that a proper conceptualisation would be necessary in order to avoid using "globalisation" as an unfounded catchphrase, as it unfortunately happens too often.

In this spirit, I am presenting a holistic, somewhat geographical, view of globalisation here, taking a cue from David Held and his colleagues who have defined globalisation as a "process ... which embodies a transformation in the spatial organization of social relations and transactions – assessed in terms of their extensity, intensity, velocity and impact – generating transcontinental or inter-regional flows and networks of activity" (Held *et al.* 1999: 16). This definition points to a restructuring of social space where flows across (internal and external) boundaries become more important in comparison with the territorial organisation of the economy and society. However, it is important to point out that this process is very uneven – manifesting itself, and affecting different places and social groups, in different ways. The project looked at the issues of *extensity, intensity and velocity*; that is, how fast and intensively social and economic relations have extended in and out of the comparatively peripheral state of Madhya Pradesh.

While globalising processes are constructed through human (everyday) action, the political-economic reforms since the announcement of the New Economic Policy in 1991 have formed particularly relevant conditions for the intensification of globalising processes that extend in to and out of regions, cities, villages and households in India. So the economists' (and our project's) attention to economic liberalisation is well justified. The project laid strong emphasis on economic actions and relations, including the role of growing exports and imports, overall commercialisation and changes in employment opportunities and their spatial patterns.

The economic reforms, however, also implied the restructuring of political spaces and changed roles for the state (and the Union

States, in particular), the private sector and civil society. Reduced transfers from the Centre, put many States under enormous fiscal stress. Some functions and responsibilities of the state also became increasingly "downloaded" to local communities and the *panchayats*, particularly after the 73rd and 74th Constitutional Amendments in 1992. To some extent, India's political decentralisation and further democratisation, therefore, needs to be understood in connection with the economic reforms.

India also experienced fast growth of (tele-)communications in the post-liberalisation period. While mobile phone and internet still have little bearing on the ordinary person in rural Madhya Pradesh (in other States this may well be very different), the increase in viewing television in Madhya Pradesh's villages has been remarkable. It is difficult to establish in how far narratives and images from serials and commercials influence cultural values or social standards, but it appears that the pace of social change has started accelerating in rural Madhya Pradesh, at times perhaps also influenced by increased spatial mobility of migrant workers.

Acknowledging these economic, political and cultural aspects of globalisation – or "glocalisation" (Swyngedouw 1997) – the research project team was particularly interested in the implications of this process for local "livelihoods". (I prefer the term *implication* in lieu of Held *et al.*'s *impact*, as it allows for the idea that everyday practices co-shape the process of globalisation producing social and economic consequences for livelihoods. The word impact, on the other hand, may fetishise globalisation and suggest simple uni-linear cause-effect relationships.)

With benefit of writing this paper after having delivered the lecture, I can respond here to one question from the audience about our own theoretical position in the globalisation debate, or the debate about the implications of globalisation. Would we see globalisation – like scholars such as Noam Chomsky – as a destructive force unleashed by those in power and subjugating ordinary men and women in the global north and south? Globalisation: the Bad. Or would we side with people like Jagdish

Bhagwati who view globalisation and markets as the redeemer of all (developmental) ills, not least in India? Globalisation: the Good. Or, finally, would we agree with Amartya Sen who laments that current institutional arrangements at global, national and local levels deny the poor the necessary social opportunities to take advantage from potential benefits of globalisation? Globalisation: the Ugly. As our applied research project aimed to find ways in which the negative implications of globalisation for the poor could be mitigated and how state and non-governmental organisations could create institutions that would enable the marginalised to better take advantage of globalising processes, we seem to fall into the camp of those who see globalisation as ugly. Our data across sectors and regions furthermore suggest that the Ugly has been resistant to become nicer. Benefits from globalisation tend to bypass the poor and marginalised sections of society in Madhya Pradesh.

3. Sustainable Livelihoods

Although not unproblematic, the concept of sustainable livelihoods posed our research team less of a challenge. Its definition is fairly undisputed, and the concept itself is very broad and all-encompassing. A livelihood is commonly regarded as sustainable "…when it can cope with and recover from stresses and shocks and maintains or enhances its capabilities and assets both now and in the future, while not undermining the natural resource base" (Carney 1998:4). We chose this dynamic concept because it pays attention to people's assets, agency and vulnerability, as well as the wider context, institutions and policies (see figure 1). People move in and out of poverty depending on their asset vulnerability and on contextual or institutional change, including globalisation and liberalisation.

While the sustainable livelihoods framework is comprehensive and nearly all-inclusive, it possesses very little explanatory power. Many factors of a livelihood are listed (some are arguably treated like a black box such as the one labelled "institutions, policies and

Figure 1: Sustainable rural livelihoods: a framework for analysis

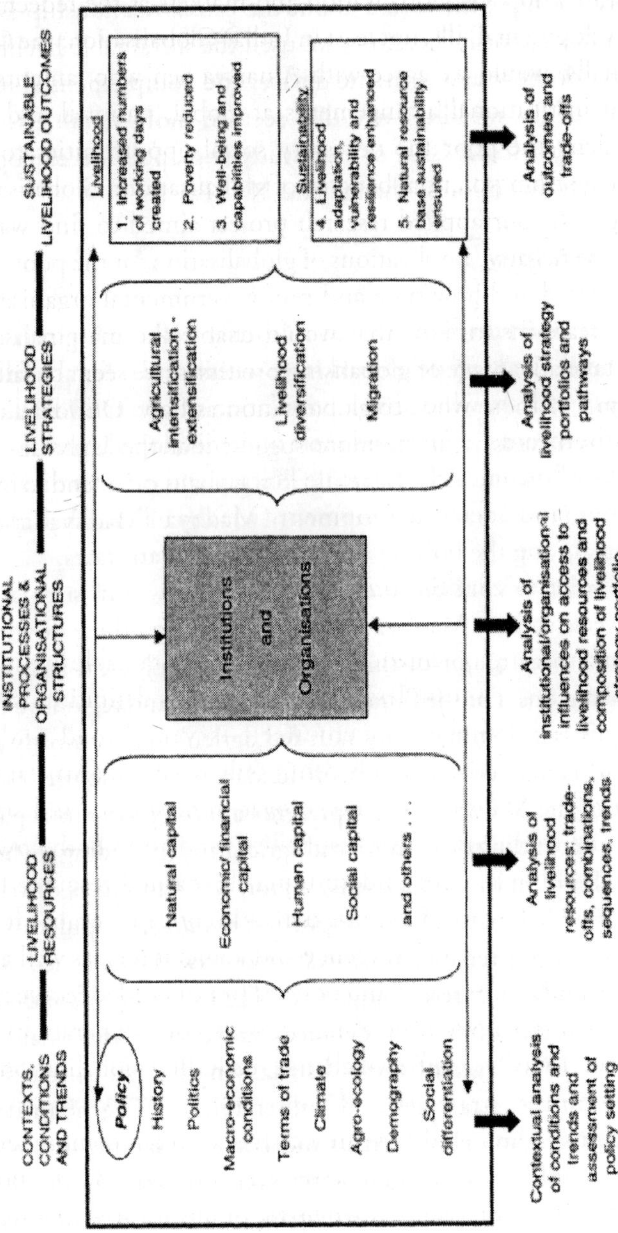

Source : Scoones (1998:4).

processes"), but little is said about the causal relationship among the various factors. Therefore, we used the sustainable livelihoods framework more as a heuristic device, and complemented it with theories of the middle range that seemed more suitable to shed light on a particular issue or case study (e.g., political ecology for the case study on forest change and NTFPs).

4. Methodology

As mentioned before, we consciously selected a relatively "peripheral" and less developed state within India for the project. Madhya Pradesh, which has a population of about 60 million, is one of the income-poorest and most underdeveloped states in India. In terms of income, HDI, female literacy and other indicators of economic and social development, Madhya Pradesh has been ranking among the bottom four of major Indian states.

In order to consider regional differences within such a large and diverse state as Madhya Pradesh, we selected three districts to represent three major distinguishable agro-ecological and socio-cultural regions. For the Bundelkhand/Bagelkhand region we chose Panna district dominated by rain-fed agriculture on mostly poor soils and characterized by a semi-feudal social structure. Sehore district in the Malwa region represents a more prosperous part of the state depending on commercial agriculture (including soybean). Finally, Betul in the Mahakoshal region was selected as district in the forested belt with a high proportion of *adivasi* population and relatively strong reliance on forest resources. That is also where this case study on forest change and NTFPs has been conducted.

The project undertook detailed quantitative and qualitative studies in 18 villages of these districts on changes in livelihood assets/resources, strategies and vulnerabilities. The quantitative study included household census and a detailed sample survey with 540 households. The qualitative research employed in-depth and semi-structured interviews, participant observation, participatory mapping methods, etc. These micro-level data sets were put in relation to secondary macro-level data on Madhya Prasesh's policy and economic changes, including trends in employment, agricultural and non-agricultural development, sectoral public expenditures, etc. As mentioned above, cross-scalar topical case studies were employed in order to better understand sector-specific interconnections between livelihoods, globalisation and reform. This was an attempt to "ground" the general research question in very concrete settings that transcend local, regional, national and global scales. For the forest change and NTFP case study, for example, information from interviews with more than 100 villagers were complemented with 22 interviews with local forest user organisations, traders and representatives of pharmaceutical companies in Nagpur and Indore, as well as with information from nine key informants in Bhopal and 22 forest officials at the state, divisional and range levels.

3. Theoretical Approach: Political Ecology

Political ecology aims to explain the interrelationship between environmental degradation and marginalisation of livelihoods by referring to political and economic factors at local, national and global scales. The attention to society-environmental relations and to various scales renders it a useful theoretical approach to analyse the implications of globalisation for forest and livelihood changes. Furthermore, political ecology is critical of simplistic explanations that take population pressure and/or the application of inappropriate technology as the underlying prime causes of environmental degradation. Instead, political ecology attempts to uncover the influence of state and market power for environmental change, and it is also sensitive to conflicting interests in particular environments or natural resources. Furthermore, this approach also overcomes the common notion of a nature-society dichotomy and sees this relationship as dialectic where society and environment are mutually dependent and co-produce one another.

A classic definition goes back to Piers Blaikie and Harold

Brookfield who wrote: "Political Ecology combines the concerns of ecology and a broadly defined political economy. Together this encompasses the constantly shifting dialectic between society and land-based resources and also within classes and groups within society itself" (1987: 17). The approach emphasizes political-economic factors for an explanation of environmental change. At the same time, it looks at the socio-political ramifications of biophysical change. Forest change in Betul district, therefore, needs to be explained not only with reference to political and economic changes at the local, but also at the state, national and global level. This could include changed state policies in the reform era as well as changing market demands at the national and global level. At the same time, political ecology demands the researcher to look at the social and political ramifications of forest change or degradation at various scales.

Furthermore, particular attention is paid to social differentiation along the lines of class, caste, gender, age, etc., and political ecology examines how access to environmental resources is socially and politically structured. Thus, conflict over the environment is a central concern and theme of political ecology. Another traditional key area of political ecology has been the investigation of the links between poverty, or "marginalisation", and environmental degradation (Robbins, 2004). Poverty or "marginalisation" is seen as both a cause and a possible consequence of environmental degradation. However, the blame is not put on the poor land users (e.g., the *adivasi* forest collector). Rather, it is acknowledged that the wider context, including the state and the world economy, forces the land users to overexploit their resources (e.g., NTFPs).

Since its classic formulation in the neo-Marxist vein of the mid-1980s, there have been theoretical advancements and new directions in political ecology. First, there has been a "cultural turn", echoing a general trend in the social sciences in the 1990s. For political ecologists, the cultural turn implied paying greater attention to the subalterns, and their diverse environmental perceptions, knowledge as well as their forms of politics ranging from unorganised passive resistance to more organised socio-environmental movements (Peet & Watts, 1996). For this research on forest change and NTFPs this implies that local forest users' diverse perceptions of degradation and their political response to it need to be analysed. Political ecology also demands a critical view of the depiction of environmental change or degradation by those in power, such as the forest officials in Madhya Pradesh.

Secondly, there has been, what has been called, a "natural turn" within political ecology. This development is in response to critiques that the field has become no more than a political economy or politics of the environment, devoid of any ecological science. Particularly geographers have therefore re-emphasised the active role of the biophysical environment, including resource characteristics, in shaping socioeconomic and political change. The biophysical environment is no longer seen simply as a passive stage where environmental conflicts play themselves out (Zimmerer & Bassett 2003). For this research this implies that the forest ecology in Betul district, as well as the resource characteristics of the studied NTFP, *safed musli*, need to be considered as active factors of environmental change and social marginalisation along – and in interaction– with the political and economic factors at various spatial scales.

4. Overview: Forest Degradation in Madhya Pradesh and in Betul District

With 76,429 sq. km forest cover, Madhya Pradesh has the largest forested area among Indian states. According to official analyses of remote sensing data, dense and open forests covers 25% of the state, and in the state's 18 tribal districts forest cover is nearly 30%; in Betul district even 35% (Forest Survey of India, 2005). On the Satpura hill range of Betul district, mainly teak forests grow– sometimes with bamboo undergrowth. Over the past ten years, forest cover has fluctuated only slightly, but there has been a relatively small reduction in the area under dense forests (Forest Survey of India, 2005). Deforestation in Betul district would have proceeded at a much faster rate prior to the 1990s, as local informants point out. This seems to be in line with the all-India trend whereby forest cover decline has been reversed particularly since the early 1990s; thanks to the increase in area under open forests.

Despite the apparent slow regeneration of forest cover, the Forest Department draws an "environmental narrative" (Leach & Mearns 1996) of a forest under constant threat by locals: "Growing demand of fuelwood and fodder is putting enormous pressure on the forest resources of the state. An area of 1.43 lakh ha is under encroachments. Forest fires take a heavy toll of the natural regeneration and forest plantation" (Forest Department, *www.forest.mp.gov.in*). At the same time, the Department depicts itself as increasingly unable to effectively protect the forest because of the advent of activist tribal mass organisations encouraging encroachments; an increase in developmental and administrative duties; as well as the ageing of its local-level staff. Therefore it would, according to the Forest Department, be "difficult to hold the staff responsible for illicit felling even in cases of dereliction of duty" (*www.forest.mp.gov.in*).

This environmental narrative also includes most officials' continued perception of the forest as a commercial timber resource. Its degradation is primarily measured in terms of forest cover change. Indeed, there is no official data collected systematically on forest quality indicators (beyond canopy density) that appear more important from the view of local forest users, as the following quote from one of our villager interviewee suggests:

> "Twenty years ago there were many trees such as *amla*, *acchar* and gums. My father depended on the sale of products from these trees [NTFPs] for the survival of the family... There are still some trees in the forest, but it is not enough for everyone. The landless can no longer rely on the forest, they have to depend on wage labour" (Field Interview).

This quote points to a perception and definition of forest degradation that is quite different from the officials' primary concern with forest cover and timber. Rather, villagers define forest degradation in direct relation to their livelihoods. Thereby, change in forest cover per se appeared only as a secondary concern, while most people commented on the loss of NTFPs (including valuable medicinal plants) from the forest near their villages. This is not very surprising, as our census of 3,000 households across Madhya Pradesh shows that the collection and sale of NTFPs still is a primary or secondary source of livelihood for about 10% of households. This figure would be higher in Betul, particularly among the poorest sections of the village communities.

Taking the perceptions and priorities of the marginalised seriously, this paper focuses on the depletion of NTFPs, in particular that of valuable medicinal plants such as *safed musli*, for the analysis of forest degradation in Madhya Pradesh. And taking another cue from political ecology, I will explain the ecological depletion of NTFPs in Betul's forests in the context of economic and political changes at other spatial scales.

5. Political-Economic Changes: Globalisation, Deregulation and Decentralisation

1. *Globalisation and Market Demand for Medicinal Plants*

The value of *safed musli* and other medicinal plants has undergone a recent transformation. While 20 years ago the plant found in central India's forests was used by local Korku and Gond communities as a salad green (leaves) and as a tonic (dried tuber), it is now marketed to pharmaceutical (allopathic, ayurvedic and homeopathic) industries domestically and abroad.

Indeed, the global demand for medicinal and herbal plant products is growing rapidly, in part because of increased consumer preference for alternative medicine in Europe and North America. In 2003, this market was estimated to account for US $ 62 billion in trade globally (WHO, 2004). Although the domestic market for these products from India remains more important (c. US$950m in 2000), exports in medicinal and herbal plants are growing very rapidly and reached US $100 million in 2000 (NMPB, 2004). It is estimated that the export growth potential still is very large, because many commercial medicinal-plant species, including *Chlorophytum borivilianum*, are endemic to India and do not grow elsewhere.

Whether domestic or international, the intensified trading of medicinal plants from forests is one of the most important ways how remote areas in Madhya Pradesh have become increasingly interconnected with the wider world. Global and national markets extend into the state's tribal villages with increased intensity and velocity. However, this increased interconnectivity has also been facilitated by various political decisions and government schemes at the national and state levels.

2. Deregulation of NTFP Marketing

The National Forest Policy of 1988 often has been depicted as a sea change in India's forest sector. Whether this is true or not is a moot point. What is important for this discussion here, however, is the increased (at least rhetorical) attention to low-volume/high-value products, including NTFPs and medicinal plants, representing a shift of focus away from soft- and hardwood timber. In the aftermath of the New Forest Policy, for example, a group of 32 medicinal-plant species have been identified by the central government as having commercial potential. These NTFPs are now supported by a Contract Farming Scheme (see 5.3).

The changed national forest policy and increased attention to valuable NTFPs has been accompanied by the state government's gradual deregulation of the forest sector since the mid-1990s. The liberalisation of Madhya Pradesh's forest sector needs to be seen as part of India's overall economic reform policy, as well as in context of a former World Bank-funded forest programme (Madhya

Pradesh Forest Programme). Of particular relevance for the NTFP and medicinal plant sector has been the "de-nationalisation" of most NTFPs. This means that the state abolished its former monopoly on the procurement of NTFPs. Previously, most NTFPs were to be collected through the primary cooperatives of the Madhya Pradesh Minor Forest Produce Federation (MPMFP) run by the Forest Department – at least in theory. Now, all NTFPs can be sold in the "open" market, except for *tendu* leaves, *sal* seeds, and tree gums, which still have to be marketed through the Forest Department. Related to the de-nationalisation of NTFPs has been the abolishment of mandatory transit permits for NTFPs in 2003. The transportation of NTFPs (except for the few nationalised ones) no longer requires the permission of the Forest Department; officers at road checkpoints no longer look for NTFPs.

The above-mentioned deregulation measures led to the freeing up of the flow of NTFPs from Madhya Pradesh's forests, and thus to an inter-regional flow of resources and activity of higher extensity, intensity and velocity – to use Held's terms. Most strikingly, this spatial transformation occurs parallel to an increased market orientation of the NTFP and medicinal plant sector that is currently supported by the National Forest Policy as well as by Madhya Pradesh's Forest Department. The state's support of an increased market orientation is perhaps better understood as an effort in re-regulating the economy than as the simple deregulation and withdrawal of the state. This is most visible in the medicinal plant sector.

3. *State Support and Re-Regulation of the Medicinal Plant Sector*

In 2000, the central government established the National Medicinal Plant Board (NMPB) with the mandate to implement and coordinate promotional and commercial schemes in India's growing medicinal plant sector. Most noteworthy has been the Contract Farming Scheme that promotes the *ex situ* cultivation of 32 commercially valuable medicinal plants (see Véron & Fehr 2006 for more detail). With the cultivation of these plants outside their natural forest habitat, the scheme hoped to achieve three objectives: (1) to stop the further impoverishment of rural people through inequitable, clandestine and opportunistic marketing of wild products, and to generate rural employment particularly in India's tribal belts; (2) to reduce the ecological pressure created by the over-harvesting of wild stocks of valuable forest plants; and (3) to increase the production of raw materials of higher quality and uniformity for the pharmaceutical industry. The Contract Farming Scheme provides cash subsidies to commercial medicinal plant growers in order to help meeting their relatively high investment and cultivation costs. Furthermore, the NMPB mediates long-term farming contracts between growers and the processing manufacturers that guarantee the producers a secure market. Unsurprisingly, the subsidies went mostly to better-off and well-connected cultivators (living in the plains) rather than to marginalised sections of society (living in the tribal hilly belt).

4. Political Decentralization

In India, the 1990s were not only characterised by economic reform and re-regulation but also by political decentralisation. First and foremost, the 73rd Constitutional Amendment of 1992 re-introduced local democratic governance in rural India through the *panchayat* system. Secondly, sector- and project-specific participatory development and resource-management programs contributed to decentralisation. Participatory decentralisation in India's forest sector even predates *panchayati raj*, and was operationalised through the Joint Forest Management (JFM) program.

Madhya Pradesh introduced JFM in 1991. Since then, reserve and protected forests are officially managed jointly by the Forest Department and local communities organised in formal committees (Forest Protection Committees and Village Forest

Committees). The idea of JFM is to provide the community a share of the benefit from the sale of forest products (including timber) in return for the protection of forests and afforested areas by the community – also referred to a "social fencing".

There is a large body of literature on JFM and its socioeconomic, political and environmental impacts in Madhya Pradesh that I do not want to rehearse here. The actual impacts, of course, differ from region to region and even from committee to committee. However, there seems to be a broad consensus that JFM in Madhya Pradesh has been fairly effective in halting or even reversing the trend of forest area decline – particularly in areas of heavily degraded forests. However, livelihood impacts seem minimal. Benefits that are supposed to be shared within the "community" are often siphoned off by forest guards and local elites who are in control of the forest committees. Furthermore, social fencing and community monitoring have in many cases even restricted local populations, particularly women, from accessing crucial forest resources such as fuelwood and fodder. Politically, JFM is said to have led to increased tensions within villages, as well as between villages bordering the same forest area. Furthermore, JFM did not lead to the political empowerment of ordinary *(adivasi)* villages, as the "participation" of local communities tends to be limited to replanting trees and safekeeping the forest, while forest-management decisions regarding tree felling, NTFP harvesting, replanting of tree and non-tree species, are still made by the forest bureaucracy. Given the environmental interests and orientations of the Forest Department, therefore, there is much emphasis on the increase of forest cover through JFM as opposed to increase incomes for the local communities.

In addition to the JFM programme, the Madhya Pradesh Panchayat Extension in Scheduled Areas (PESA) Act of 1996 forms an important part of political decentralisation in the forest sector. Indeed, the nominal ownership of all forest products has been transferred to the local *gram sabhas* and *gram panchayats*. On the ground, however, little appears to have changed. *De facto* control over forest resources remains with the Forest Department. This is particularly the case for timber from forest areas, for which the state keeps the monopoly for procurement. What was in the past termed the Forest Department's "share" of benefits is now simply relabelled as their "management fee".

The recent initiatives of decentralisation created an institutional complexity at the local level with JFM committees, *gram sabhas* and MFPFED primary cooperatives officially having a stake in the management and control of (non-timber) forest resources. However, the activities of these formal local institutions are largely uncoordinated and their respective functions are overlapping to some extent. Rather than representing institutional alternatives for poor people depending on forest resources, these institutions remained ineffective in strengthening sustainable forest-based livelihoods. Nevertheless, and perhaps ironically, the formal decentralised bodies may also have allowed the state (as well as globalising processes) to extend deeper into remote forest areas in Madhya Pradesh.

6. Socio-Spatial and Environmental Processes

1. The Tuber: Safed Musli

I discuss some recent and fairly common socio-spatial and environmental processes related to Madhya Pradesh's forests with the example of *safed musli*. *Chlorophytum borivilianum* grows a valuable tuber. Its active ingredient saponin is responsible for the tonic and energising qualities of the plant. The dried tuber is included in many natural medicine products and has for long been used to treat diabetes and arthritis. *Safed musli* is also alleged to be an aphrodisiac and, indeed, it is in some places marketed as "natural Viagra". Like many other medicinal plants from India, it has a growing domestic and local market demand. It also belongs to the 32 plants selected by the NMPB for commercial development.

Chlorophytum borivilianum grows naturally in the semi-deciduous forests of Southern Rajasthan, Northern Gujarat and Madhya Pradesh. However, the plant lends itself to be cultivated in open fields. It is mostly propagated vegetatively by rhizome but also by seed. In fields, the tubers can be harvested after 3-4 months. These botanical characteristics, together with the changes in the political-economic context and the activities of tribal collectors, traders and officials shaped particular socio-spatial as well as environmental processes that are described below using a case study from a village in Chicholi block, Betul district.

2. *The View from a Village*

In our extensive study of a village in Chicholi block we discovered a rapid process of commodification and resource depletion of *Chlorophytum borivilianum* (as well as other NTFPs that have recently gained in market value). Before the 1990s, *safed musli* was only occasionally collected by Korku women and they consumed it as a salad green and sometimes also as a dried tonic. In 1992, however, non-tribal traders from Chicholi town coming to the village started buying the white tuber. The sale of *safed musli* increased steadily. By 1999, *adivasi* and OBC people of the entire village were involved in the collection of this medicinal plant. The town-based traders would park their jeeps on the road in the forest, and wait for the local collectors to come out and sell *safed musli*. This was also the year when prices peaked, but stocks of this NTFP started dwindling due to over-harvesting. A significant change was observed in 2001 when small, wet rhizome tubers started to be sold in significant numbers. This harmed the regenerative capacity of the wild stock further, as *Chlorophytum borivilianum* propagates mostly vegetatively in nature. Sadly, in 2004 the forest in the vicinity of the villages was completely emptied of this valuable plant. Only a very few Korku men were still involved in the collection of *safed musli* deep in the forest and very far from the village.

3. *Market Changes and Commercial Cultivation*

Globalisation and gradual liberalisation of the NTFP sector represent part of the relevant political-economic context of the observed processes of commodification of *safed musli* and other NTFPs. In the absence of (effective) community-based or state-controlled resource management that would regulate the access, collection and trade of this valuable species, the increasing global prices and a "free" market could easily lead to the overexploitation of the resource. To researchers of tribal India, furthermore, it will not be surprising that even the short-term benefits from the commodification and globalisation of *safed musli* did not "trickle down" substantially to the *adivasi* forest collectors. In this like in other cases, historical power relationships reproduced the economic exploitation of the forest collectors and their environment, as the simplified representation of the commodity chain in figure 2 indicates. The commodity chain of *safed musli* from Chicholi block is very long and exploitative (as in the case of most other valuable NTFPs): while forest collectors received Rs.350-400 per kg dried *safed musli* in 1996, the same product achieved Rs. 1,200 in Indore. Still, from the perspective of the poor *adivasi*, the collection of the tuber was very profitable – enough to form a strong economic incentive to engage in this activity.

However, the tale of tribals, traders and *safed musli* is more complex. Around 2001, the commodity chain from our study villages began to be altered (see figure 3) as the commercial cultivation of the tuber near Chicholi town became substantial. In 1998, two non-tribal farmers from the town started experimenting with the cultivation of *Chlorophytum borivilianum*. They got to know – possibly through manufacturers from Indore – about the scientific cultivation methods recommended by a government research station in Rajasthan. Two other cultivators also received subsidies under the Contract Farming Scheme in the early 2000s. This had a further demonstration effect on local farmers (but also teachers and businessmen) to start growing *safed musli* on own and rented land. By 2004, more than 20 cultivators were growing this medicinal plant on fields near Chicholi town. Due to very high input costs, the commercial cultivation of *safed musli* has been limited to resource-rich (exclusively non-tribal) people, but at least between 1998 and 2002, it reaped very high returns.

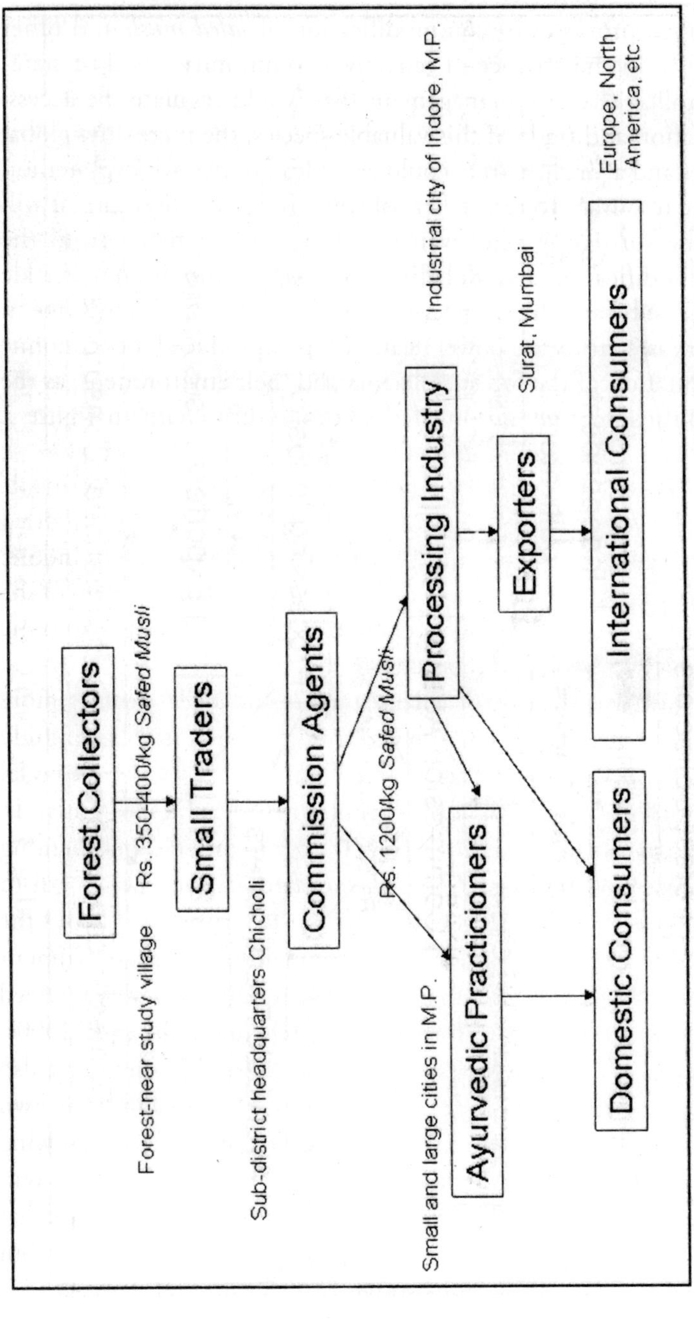

Fig. 2 : *Safed Musli* Commodity Chain, c. 1996

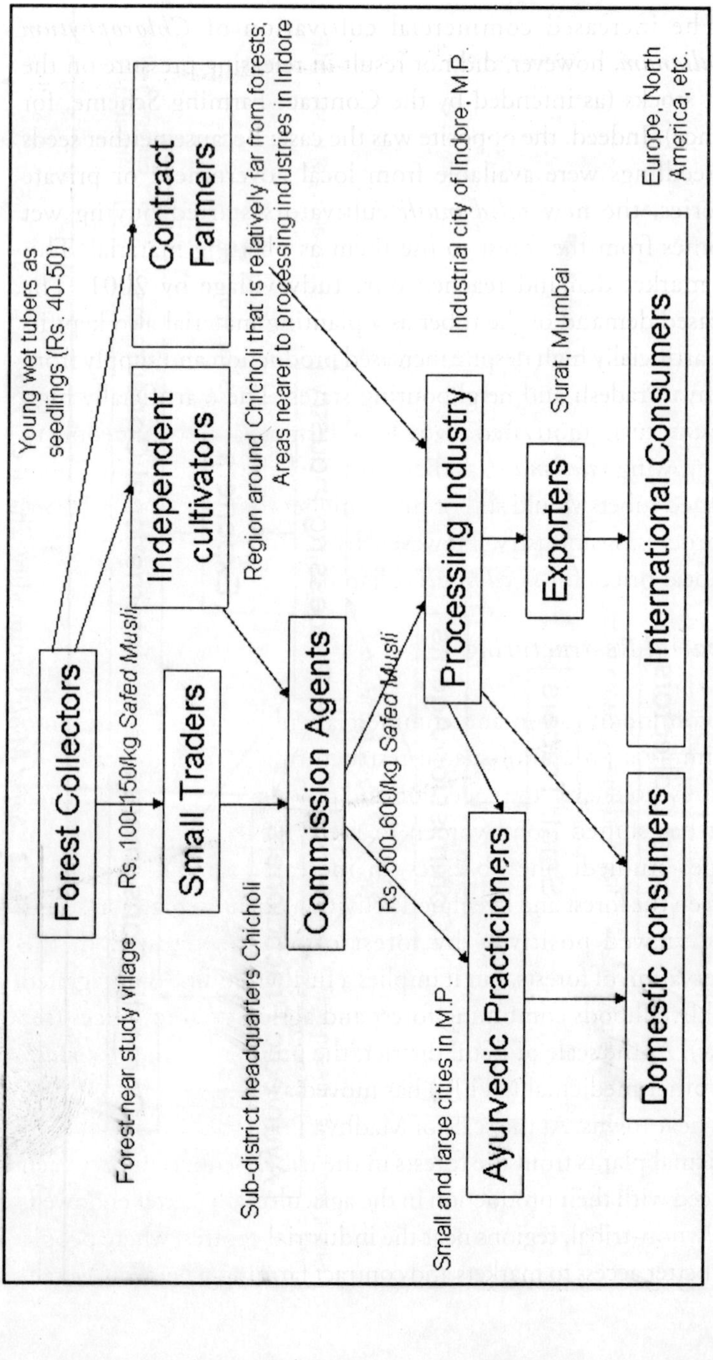

Fig. 3: *Safed Musli* Commodity Chain, c. 2003

The increased commercial cultivation of *Chlorophytum borivilianum*, however, did not result in releasing pressure on the forest stocks (as intended by the Contract Farming Scheme, for instance). Indeed, the opposite was the case: Because neither seeds nor seedlings were available from local government or private nurseries, the new *safed musli* cultivators started buying wet rhizomes from the forest to use them as planting material. This new market demand reached our study village by 2001. The increased demand of the tuber as a planting material also kept its price artificially high despite increased production and supply from Madhya Pradesh and neighbouring states. These artificially high prices, in turn, motivated many local farmers and town people to start growing *safed musli*, as they wrongly believed that demand of the dried tubers would still be much higher than the demand from the processing industry. However, by c. 2003 the bubble burst, and local prices for *safed musli* collapsed.

4. Spatial Restructuring

The commodification and commercial cultivation of *safed musli* also imply a process of spatial restructuring at various scales. At the household level, the collection and production of this medicinal plant has shifted from women to men. At the level of the two villages studied, one observes an increased spatial separation between the forest and livelihood activities. Such a separation seems to be viewed positively by forest officials interested in the conservation of forests, but it implies a further decline of integrated tribal livelihoods combining forest and agricultural resources (see below). At the scale of Betul district, the production of *safed musli* (and other medicinal NTFPs) has moved away from the forests to areas near towns. At the scale of Madhya Pradesh, the collection of medicinal plants from the forests in the tribal belt has in part been replaced with their production in the agriculturally better endowed, largely non-tribal, regions near the industrial centres, where people have better access to markets and contract farming schemes. Overall, this case study shows how the remote study village in Chicholi block has become increasingly interconnected to the wider world through economic relations – yet not on its own terms.

5. Implications for Sustainable Livelihoods

The depletion of forest resources such as *Chlorophytum borivilianum* and other valuable species fortunately did not lead to a widespread livelihood crisis in Betul's forest-near villages. Rather, local people had already shifted away from forest-based livelihoods before *Chlorophytum borivilianum* vanished from the forests. This may in part be due to the prior gradual degradation of NTFPs and the long history of people's exclusion from forest resources by colonial and post-colonial forest policies. Most important in Betul district, however, has been the emergence of new income opportunities through the rapid growth of irrigated agriculture and seasonal migration since the early 1990s. Respondents generally favoured the work in agricultural fields in the village and elsewhere, and they did not share any romantic notions of roaming through forests to collect NTFPs. The collection of *safed musli*, though very lucrative for some time, was for most people a side occupation and their behaviour can be interpreted as largely opportunistic.

Nevertheless, the exhaustion of this natural asset has implications for *sustainable* livelihoods, in particular for the possibility for livelihood diversification and the vulnerability of the poorest of the poor for whom the collection of NTFPs is still important. For example, elderly women – who are physically not fit enough to be employed on the fields or to migrate – find it increasingly difficult to contribute to the household income because of the depletion of NTFPs in the vicinity of their houses. Also, in times of economic crises or "shocks" (e.g., droughts), the local population can no longer depend on *safed musli* and other valuable NTFPs as a last resort.

The commercial cultivation of medicinal plants, on the other hand, failed to create employment for former (tribal) forest collectors. The commercial fields are far from their villages and forests, and the cultivators tend to employ local non-tribals on their fields. Generally, medicinal-plant cultivation and harvests do not require much labour. *Safed musli* even seems to have failed the more prosperous cultivators. In expectation of high returns, many took on big loans to cover the very high cultivation costs and now, after the price collapse, they find themselves unable to repay.

7. Concluding Remarks

This case study can be seen as an attempt to "ground" somewhat aloof ideas of globalisation in real world contexts. It showed how globalising processes – supported by liberalisation policies and the state promotion of valuable medicinal plants –transformed economic relations across space and created an intensified inter-regional flow of resources and commodities. In the case of *safed musli*, globalisation shows its ugly face and implied the continued, perhaps enhanced, exploitation of tribal forest collectors and the depletion of local forest resources. These processes also have been enabled and pronounced by the particular ecological characteristics of *Chlorophytum borivilianum*: The rhizomes of young tubers can be used as planting material, yet this practice also harms the regenerative capacity of the wild stock. Indeed, the specific socio-spatial and environmental processes analysed in this paper have been co-produced by particular global and domestic market demands, government policies and schemes, local power relations, ecological characteristics of the product and the region, and their interplay. The trajectory of globalisation may be very different for other valuable NTFPs in other regions. Therefore it is needless to say that generalisations cannot be drawn from this case study.

In the question-and-answer section of my presentation at Vidyasagar University, one participant rightly pointed out that politics were largely missing from this supposedly *political*-ecological analysis of globalisation and sustainable livelihoods. Indeed, the analysis of the politics surrounding globalisation, India's liberalisation policies or even the Contract Farming Scheme was beyond the scope of this research. The project deliberately excluded that question. However, this case study considered, following the "cultural turn" of political ecology, the political agency of the forest collectors whether in organized forms or through acts of passive resistance. However, the depletion of valuable NTFPs and the dislocation of forest-based livelihoods turned out to be little politicised in Madhya Pradesh. Tribal Mass Organisations, which are very active in the area of land rights, for instance, seem not to have picked up this issue. Therefore, this study is perhaps less about *politics* (or the decision-making about and conflicts around resource access and benefits) and more about *the political*, or the power inherent in environment-society relationships at different spatial scales. In this way, I hope that I was still able to stay true to the premise of political ecology that sees relationships between society and environment as dialectical and laden with power.

Foot-Note

1. This collaborative project entitled "Globalisation and the Poor: Sustaining Rural Livelihoods in India" was conducted jointly by the Jawaharlal Nehru University, the Centre for Social Development, Delhi, and the University of Guelph. The project was funded from 2003-2005 by the Canadian International Development Agency (CIDA) as one of 19 sub-projects of the Shastri Indo-Canadian Institute Applied Research Project (SHARP). The views expressed here, however, are my own and not necessarily those of CIDA. For the case study on *safed musli* I draw heavily on data collected by my PhD student Garry Fehr, who however is not responsible for possible errors in interpretation.

References

Blaikie P. & Brookfield, H. (1987) *Land Degradation and Society*, London: Methuen.

Carney, D. (1998) *Sustainable Rural Livelihoods: What Contribution Can We Make?* London: DFID.

Forest Survey of India (2005) *Forest Survey of India, 2003*, Dehradun: MoEF.

Held, D., McGrew, A., Goldblatt, D. & Perraton, J. (1999) *Global Transformations. Economics, Politics and Culture*, Cambridge: Polity Press.

Leach, M. & Mearns, R (eds.) (1996) *The Lie of the Land: Challenging Received Wisdom in African Environmental Change and Policy*, Oxford: James Currey.

NMPB (2004) National Medicinal Plants Board. Available at www.nmpb.nic.in.

Peet R. & Watts, M. (eds.) (1996) *Liberation Ecologies: Environment, Development, and Social Movements*, London: Routledge.

Robbins, P. (2004) *Political Ecology: A Critical Introduction*, London: Blackwell.

Scoones, I. (1998) "Sustainable Rural Livelihoods: A Framework for Analysis", IDS Working Paper 72. Brighton: Institute of Development Studies.

Swyngedouw, E. (1997) "Neither Global nor Local: 'Glocalization' and the Politics of Scale", in Cox, K.R. (ed.) *Spaces of Globalization: Reasserting the Power of the Local*, New York: Guilford Press, pp. 137-166.

Véron, R. & Fehr, G. (2006) "Unintended Consequences: Ex-Situ Cultivation of Medicinal Plants and Forest Resource Depletion in Madhya Pradesh' *Inform* 5(1).

WHO (2004) World Health Organization. Available at www.who.int/en.

Zimmerer, K.S. & Bassett, T.J. (eds.) 2003 *Political Ecology: An Integrative Approach to Geography and Environment-Development Studies*, New York: Guilford.

3 Human Undernutrition : Two Serious Challenges

Dilip Mahalanabis

I

THE PROBLEM OF LOW BIRTH WEIGHT IN INDIA

Seventy percent of the annual 32 million low birth weight (LBW, weight <2.5 kg at birth) neonates globally are born in developing countries (UNICEF, 2004). In South Asia (includes India) an estimated 30 percent of the babies born are of low birth weight (UNICEF, 2004).

Low Birth Weight (LBW)

Country	*LBW Rate*
India	30%
Bangladesh	30%
Sri Lanka	22%
USA	08%

LBW is often used as a proxy indicator for intrauterine growth retardation (IUGR) in developing countries because a valid assessment of gestational age is often not available. It is estimated that two thirds of the low birth weight babies in India are due to IUGR (NNF, India, 2001).

Definitions

LBW	:	Birth Weight <2500 g
Premature	:	Infants born before 37 weeks gestation
Intrauterine Growth Retardation (IUGR)	:	Weight <10th percentile for pregnancy duration

LBW is associated with increased morbidity and mortality, impaired immune function, and poor cognitive development (Ashworth A, 1998) for neonates, infants and young children. The risk of neonatal deaths among babies weighing 2 to 2.5 kg at birth was estimated to be four times the rate in neonates with birth weight of 2.5 to 3 kg and ten times higher than in neonates weighing 3 to 3.5 kg (Ashworth A, 1998). Of all the neonatal deaths in India, an estimated 81% occur among LBW neonates and a high proportion of neonatal deaths occur among pre-term babies (NNF, India, 2001).

Risk of Neonatal Death in Low Birth Weight Babies

-BW 2 kg to <2.5 kg VS 2.5 kg to <3 kg	4 folds increase
-BW 2kg to 2.5kg VS 3 kg to <3.5 kg	10 folds increase

Determinants of LBW in Developing Countries

Maternal under nutrition:

- Low gestational weight gain
- Low per-pregnancy body mass index (BMI)
- Short maternal stature
- Micronutrient deficiencies

Other etiologic determinants:

- Young maternal age (adolescent)
- Malaria during pregnancy
- Gastro-intestinal, respiratory, intestinal Parasitosis, and/or other infections
- Cigarette smoking

Recent findings (Barker DJP & Colleagues) on the relationship between intrauterine growth retardation (IUGR) and diseases in adults such as hypertension, type II diabetes, coronary heart disease generated renewed interest in studying the developmental indicators of infants and young children (Barker DJP et al., 1995, 1998). Barker DJP and colleagues and Lucas A and Singhal A have further shown that more rapid postnatal growth (catch-up growth) in infants born with IUGR plays an important role on the risk of these adult diseases (Erikson, Barker DJP et al., 1999 and Singhal A. Lucas A, 2004). In South Asian countries the rate of low birth weight (LBW) is very high largely due to intrauterine growth retardation. Further, the incidence of hypertension, type II diabetes and coronary heart disease is high among South Asian compared to the Caucasians (C.S.Yajnik et al., 2002). High incidence of low birth weight in India therefore, assumes great public health importance.

The rate of low birth weight is very high in India. In contrast, it is substantially lower in many African countries. Low birth weight of a girl child along with nutritional deprivation in childhood and adolescence leads to a under weight and stunted woman as an adult. Such a woman is likely to give birth to babies with low birth weight, thus completing a life cycle of malnutrition. Some health experts proposed a life cycle approach to address this important health and nutrition problem. However some practical interventions may still be thought of to assist in reducing the incidence of low birth weight. They include, a) preventing pregnancy in quick succession (i.e. birth spacing), b) deferring pregnancy until after adolescence (i.e. prevention of teen age pregnancy), c) good nutrition throughout life cycle, and d) high energy antenatal diet supplement. While low birth weight is known to be associated with high mortality and morbidity in infancy and early childhood, a new dimension has been added to this problem by David Barker who proposed the "fetal origin of adult disease" hypothesis in 1989 (Barker 1989).

Further, Yajnik and colleagues from Pune have shown that babies with low birth weight have proportionately much more reduced lean body mass (i.e. mainly bones, muscles and viscera) and fat mass is relatively preserved. These investigators categorised this phenomenon as 'thin fat' baby syndrome. Association of small size of a baby at birth (largely a proxy for intra-uterine growth retardation) and subsequently accelerated growth rate in infancy and childhood with adult disease like coronary heart disease, type II diabetes and hypertension has led to new interest and research initiatives on intra-uterine growth retardation.

II
MICRONUTRIENT DEFICIENCY

Many micronutrients are known to be essential in the human diet; but only three of them – vitamin A, iron and iodine are accepted to be commonly deficient and global intervention programmes have been launched to combat their deficiency. In addition, folate supplementation during pregnancy is also included among the essential public health measures largely to prevent congenital anomalies. However, there is a growing body of evidence that zinc might also be included in this category. Micronutrient deficiencies are manifested by a group of distorts that have serious health, social and economic costs to society. I propose to discuss iron deficiency as an example of an important micronutrient deficiency of Public Health importance.

Iron Deficiency

Iron is a constituent of hemoglobin and some enzymes and electron carriers, and it is obtained from food. Iron deficiency is the most common form of malnutrition in the world, affecting more than 1.3 billion people globally. Prevalence of iron deficiency anemia is very high in developing countries but also remains a problem in developed countries. There are other causes of anemia such as due to vitamin B_{12} and folate deficiency and heredity (e.g. thalassemia). However, in countries with high prevalence of anemia, iron deficiency is usually the most common cause. Blood hemoglobin or hematocrit values are commonly used to assess the severity of anemia in a population (Table-3.1).

Table 3.1*: Hemoglobin and hematocrit cutoffs to define anemia in people living at sea level

Group		*Hemoglobin below (g/dl)*	*Hematocrit below (%)*
Children	: 6m-5yr	11.0	33
	: 5yr-11yr	11.5	34
	: 12yr-13yr	12.0	36
Non-pregnant Women		12.0	36
Men		13.0	39

* From WHO/UNICEF/UNU, 1997

Magnitude of the Problem

As stated earlier about 1.3 billion people suffer form iron deficiency anemia (United Nations 1990). The age and physiological status determine the degree of vulnerability of the individual: rapidly growing infants, children, and pregnant and lactating women are at high risk for deficiency.

Table-3.2*

Country	*Prevalence of Anemia (%)*[+]			
	0-4 yr	*5-12yr*	*Men (15-49yr)*	*All Women (15-49yr)*
South Asia (Includes India)	56%	50%	32%	58%
Africa	56%	49%	20%	44%
Latin America	26%	26%	13%	18%

* DeMaeyer and Adiels-Tegman,1985

Psychological Development

Iron deficiency anemia (IDA) in infants and young children is associated with significantly lower scores on psychological tests (Pollitt, 1993a; Lozoff et al., 1991; Lozoff, 1998). Pollitt noted that deficits of 0.5 to 1.5 standard deviation units in scores on infant development scales or IQ tests of children have been found quite consistently across studies and age groups. Moreover, these effects of iron deficiency anemia during infancy are associated with lower development test scores at 5 years of age (Lozoff et al., 1991) and have been shown to have effects during school age in studies in France, Israel, and the U.S. (summarized in Lozoff, 1998), even controlling for other differences between children and families. Studies of less severe iron depletion have found psychological impairment less consistently (Idjradinata and Pollitt, 1993; Soewondo et al., 1989).

How iron deficiency affects psychological development is under debate. There may be direct effects on brain development. Iron supplementation interventions that successfully improve the iron status of infants and young children with iron-deficiency anemia can improve performance on tests of psychological development, although not always to the level of children who have not suffered anemia.

INTERVENTIONS

Iron Supplements

In many populations as in India, the amount of iron absorbed from the diet is not sufficient to meet many individuals' requirements. This is especially likely to be true during infancy and pregnancy, when physiological iron requirements are the highest. If the amount of absorbable iron in the diet cannot be immediately improved, iron supplementation will be a necessary component of programs to control iron deficiency anemia. This will almost always be the case for children 6-24 months of age and pregnant women. The priority among target groups for iron supplementation is based on the likelihood of both iron deficiency and the public health benefits resulting from its control. Pregnant and postpartum women and children 6-24 months of age are the priority target groups for both reasons.

Food-based Interventions

Fortification of suitable food vehicles with absorbable forms of iron is highly desirable approach to controlling iron deficiency. If a fortifiable food exists that is consumed by many people at risk of iron deficiency, fortification is likely to be the most cost-effective component of its control. There are many possible strategies for iron fortification. One approach is to fortify a staple food that is consumed in significant quantities by most of the population. Fortification of wheat flour with iron is technically relatively simple and this has been successfully implemented in several countries in the Caribbean, South America. North America, and Great Britain. Another approach is to fortify a widely consumed condiment. Fish sauce, curry powder, salt, and sugar have all been successfully fortified with iron. In South America, both dried and liquid milk and milk products such as yogurt have been fortified with iron.

Helminth Control

Where hookworm infection is endemic (prevalence 20-30% or higher) and anemia is very prevalent, hookworm infection is likely to be an important cause of anemia, especially moderate-to-severe anemia. Hookworms (*Necator americanus* and *Ancylostoma duodenale*) infect approximately 1 billion of the world's population, an estimated 44 million of whom are pregnant women. In populations with endemic hookworm, anthelminthic therapy should be given presumptively to anyone with severe anemia, because treatment is safe and much less expensive than diagnosing hookworm infection. Anthelminthic treatment to school children without prior screening is currently recommended in the school setting and combined with iron-folate supplementation in antenatal care.

Malaria Control

Plasmodium falciparum malaria causes a profound anemia during and after acute infection. The anemia is caused by hemolysis of red cells combined with suppression of erythropoiesis.

Consequently, body iron is shifted from hemoglobin to storage forms. Where *Plasmodium falciparum* malaria is endemic, the use of insecticide-impregnated bed nets in communities decreases the prevalence of severe anemia in young children.

Reproductive and Obstetric Interventions

Preventing adolescent pregnancies, reducing the total number of pregnancies, and increasing the time between pregnancies will also contribute to the control of iron deficiency anemia in women. Obstetrical practices can also contribute to the control of iron deficiency anemia in infants. More red blood cells are transferred from the placenta to the newly born infant if the umbilical cord is not clamped and legated until it stops pulsating.

Role of Applied Research Programmes

Experience has shown that programmes to control anemia and other forms of malnutrition are most successful in countries where they are supported by one or more teams of researchers dedicated to carrying out applied research related to nutrition interventions. A few noteworthy examples are Chile, Argentina, and Venezuela in the control of anemia and Indonesia and Guatemala in the control of vitamin A deficiency.

REFERENCES

A Critical Link: Interventions for physical growth and psychological development. *A Review*, Department of Child and Adolescent Health and Development, World Health Organization: WHO/CHS/CAH/99.3.

Ashworth A. Effects of intrauterine growth retardation on mortality and morbidity in infants and young children. Eur J Clin Nutr 1998; 42(Suppl 1): S34-S42.

Barker DJP. Fetal origins of coronary heart disease. BMJ 1995; 311: 171-174.

Barker DJP. Mohers, Babies and Health in Adult Life. Edinburgh: Churchill Livingstone. 1998.

Disease Control Priorities in Developing Countries: edited by Jamison DT, Mosley WH, Measham AR, Bobadilla JL. *Published by Oxford University Press*, New York. 1993

Eriksson JG, Forsen T, Tuomilehto J, Osmond C, Barker DJ. Early adiposity rebound in childhood and risk of type-2 diabetes in adult life. Diabetologies 2003;46:190-194.

Lozoff B, Jimenez E, Wolf AW. Long-term developmental outcomes of infants with iron deficiency. *New England Journal of Medicine*, 1991, 325:687-694.

Lozoff B. Explanatory mechanisms for poorer development in iron-deficient anemic infants. In: *Nutriion, health, and child development: research advances and policy recommendations.* Pan American Health Organization, Tropical Metabolism Research Unit of the University of the West Indies, and The World Bank. Scientific Publication 566, 1998:162-178.

National Neonatology Forum, India. *National Neonatal Perinatal Database: report for the year 2000.* New Delhi, National Neonatology Forum, India, 2001:13-38.

Pollitt E. Iron deficiency and cognitive function. *Annual Reviews of Nutrition*, 1993a, 13:521-537.

Singhal A, Lucas A. Early Origins of cardiovascular disease: is there a unifying hypothesis? *Lancet* 2004; 363: 1642-1645.

United Nations Children's Fund. The State of the World's Children 2004, New York: United Nations Children's Fund, 2004:100-113.

Yajnik CS, Lubree HG, Rege SS, Naik SS, Deshpande JA, Deshpande SS et al.: Adiposity and Hyperinsulinemia in Indians Are Present at birth. *The Journal of Clinical Endocrinology & Metabolism* 2002;12:5575-5580.

4 The Mainstream and the Margin

Tribal Policy and Administration in India and Southern Africa

Ansu Datta

Introduction

In any society, much of the problem of social integration centres on relations between what are generally labelled as the centre and the periphery, the mainstream and the margin. The present essay seeks to offer, on a comparative basis, two ways in which the problem is addressed in India and southern Africa. In doing this, we have not merely examined the 'symmetricality' and equivalence of such relationships, but have, in addition, raised the question of the identity of the mainstream. In this exercise, we note that while in India the identity of the mainstream is unquestioned, in southern Africa, the notion of the mainstream has been undergoing qualitative transformation, given the changes occurring in the power equation obtaining in different countries of the region.

We start with the assertion that one of the most appropriate ways to conceptualise the two sections, the mainstream and the margin, is in terms of power that they command and wield. The marginalised are the communities that were historically isolated and are even now disadvantaged in different ways. The history of India is in a sense the history of the many attempts made at adjustment between the margin and the mainstream, the full story of which is yet to be told. In the context of the immense ethnic diversity, there is no reason to pose a unilinear path of these experiments leading to a revision of the equation between the two sections. The Data on People of India (Singh, 1989) identified as many as 4,384 communities in all states/union territories including 426 Scheduled Tribes, 443 Scheduled Castes, and 1,051 Backward Classes. With the politicisation of much of Indian social life and owing to the onset and strengthening of the democratic process, some on the margin are making a bid to establish a new kind of *modus vivendi* with the mainstream at a different level.

Three models of such adjustment are apparent. In the first place are the so-called 'tribal' peoples, in segmentary linkage to the mainstream. These roughly correspond to the communities listed under the category, *Scheduled Tribes*. Then there are the *Scheduled Castes* or *dalits*, in a delicately balanced organic linkage to the mainstream, especially to its principal constituent, the Hindu social order. The third model stands for part of the same in a conspicuously rebellious mode, projecting an organic but alternative relationship to the mainstream. The three models of the marginalised peoples sustain three contrasting types of responses to the continued dominance of the mainstream, depending on their linkage, however tenuous, to the mainstream. Strictly speaking, the underprivileged and deprived *social classes* too are marginalised. However, in this essay we have decided not to discuss the social class aspect of marginalization.

Although directed by the mainstream, the Indian state apparatus is making some efforts, even if half-hearted, to bring the marginalised communities to the democratic process. A question remains as to the effectiveness of these measures to change the power equation in society. Power relations are reflected in all facets of public life, education, health, employment, etc. This paper argues that the democratic system as it prevails in India emerges from the negotiations that the mainstream and the marginalised carry out; indeed, the system turns itself into an arena where further interaction between them takes place.

In the Indian context, tribal groups are identified administratively, if only because they are listed officially under the title 'the Scheduled Tribes'. The country's constitution (Art. 46) enjoins the state 'to promote the educational and economic interests of the Scheduled Tribes, along with other 'weaker sections' of the population' and 'to protect them from social injustice and all forms of exploitation'. One important way in which the Indian mainstream has tried to achieve this objective is by providing for extensive reservation for them in political representation, employment, housing and admission to educational institutions.

However, the realisation that privileges extended to the Scheduled Tribes are being 'cornered' by the bigger, better organised and more advanced tribes has led to the preparation of a list of 'Primitive Tribal Groups' (PTGs) who are entitled to more favoured treatment. Currently, this list includes 75 such communities from 15 states and Union Territories. PTGs are identified on the following criteria: (1) stagnant or decreasing population, (2) literacy below two percent, and (3) technologically backward economy based on shifting cultivation and collection of minor forest products. Unfortunately, beyond the provision for a special grant, it is not clear how far the 'separate plan of action' for PTGs is inspired by a distinctive approach.

In southern Africa, there were and still are different shades of marginality. With 'the wind of change' blowing over Africa, several former marginalised groups such as various Bantu-speaking black communities have shed off some degree of their marginality and have entered into the ranks of the mainstream or are in the process of doing so. In this essay, we will focus mainly on the Khoisan peoples as an illustration of one of the most marginalised peoples in the region.

The term Khoisan in the present context includes both the Khoi Khoi (the so-called Hottentots) and various San (the so-called Bushmen) communities. They are easily distinguished from the peoples of the European stock and black Africans, who speak various Bantu languages including Setswana and who, at least in Botswana, are referred to as 'the black people' by the San.

A comparison of the position of the Khoisan peoples of

southern Africa and of the so-called tribal peoples of India including an account of how they are administered, and consequently, what their current statuses are, centre on the main thrust of the problematique of this paper. First, both India and southern Africa demonstrate a great variety of human types in terms of culture, kinship, religion, language, and technological and productive level achieved, from the stone age to the nuclear age. One of the main problems of development that the governments and other institutions of the establishment of these regions face is how best to bridge the gulf between communities at different levels of development and integration. The commonality of the predicament consists in either case of the same confusion at the policy level. Policy makers and those who implement policies show the same propensity to indulge in generalities and similar inertia to apply them meaningfully to concrete situations. Nehru's Panchsheel[(1)] and Verrier Elwin's National Park theory are, in their sterile idealism, comparable to what administrations in Botswana and Namibia attempted or claimed to have attempted. This is appropriately illustrated by the inept efforts made by administrative authorities in southern Africa to create 'reservations' for the Khoisan. The designation of NyaeNyae, a constituent region in Namibia, as 'Bushmanland' where local administration enjoys certain powers goes only partly to administrative decentralisation.

Sadly, in South Africa, most Khoisan have become extinct culturally, before any well-coordinated policy could be rationally thought out, let alone enforced consistently and systematically. In fact, this was not a relevant issue to those who ruled the country at different levels and in diverse garbs since 1652 until the country's liberation in 1994[(2)].

India obviously is much larger in area than any of the southern African countries where Khoisan peoples live. If, however, we take together the combined area of Angola, Botswana, Namibia and South Africa, the region is larger than India (3.8 m sq. km as opposed to 3.2 m sq. km). Likewise, the Scheduled Tribes in India constitute 6.5 per cent of the total population. This, according to the 1961 Census of India, numbered more than thirty million people in absolute terms. The Khoisan population, on the other hand, is just about 3 per cent of southern Africa's population. The Khoisan peoples and the Scheduled Tribes in India are both dispersed over a wide area. In terms of identity, just as it is not possible to bracket the entire Khoisan peoples as one group with a sufficiently strong feeling of solidarity, similarly the Scheduled Tribes are divided into many separate communities. The South African government established in May 1999 the National Khoisan Council (*South African Yearbook 2002/03*: 313) to deal collectively with common problems that face Khoisan peoples; however, it is too early to say how far the Council can contribute to the shaping of a common identity among various Khoisan groups.

One special difficulty in identifying a tribal group in the Indian context is its dynamic relations to the local caste-based society. In the ongoing process of integration, it is not always easy to judge whether a group has attained the status of a *jati* in the local caste-based system or remains a tribal social system. The process of interaction itself assumes a variety of different forms, from complete isolation at one extreme to full assimilation on the other with several intermediate stages between them.

In constitutional matters, the Scheduled Tribes are better placed in India than the Khoisan are in southern Africa. Part XVI (Special Provisions Relating to Certain Classes) of the Indian Constitution sets out the manner in which matters relating to the Scheduled Castes and Scheduled Tribes are to be addressed. India has as many as eight States with a clear majority of the locally dominant tribe(s) (Cf. Fourth Schedule of the Constitution with amendments[(4)]). Additionally, the Constitution recognizes at least one 'tribal' language, Santali, for certain official purposes. Members of Scheduled Tribes have been holding important positions in the central cabinet and bureaucracy, and have gone abroad as the country's diplomatic representatives. In socioeconomic development, the Scheduled Tribes have made much greater progress than the Khoisan in southern Africa, as is evident from Table 4.1.

Table 4.1: Human Development[(3)] in Six North-Eastern States of India Dominated by Scheduled Tribes

	% of Population below Poverty line 1999-2000	*Adult Literacy Rate 1995-96*	*Under-5 Mortality Rate 1991*	*Human Development Index (1991)*
Arunachal Pradesh	33.47	44.54	139	0.300
Manipur	28.54	64.49	39	0.503
Meghalaya	33.87	77.09	98	0.332
Mizoram	19.47	88.43	68	0.464
Nagaland	32.67	80.87	67	0.442
Sikkim	36.56	63.89	85	0.425
All India average	26.10	54.32	94	0.381

Source : Planning Commission, Government of India (2002) *National Human Development Report 2001*. Oxford. Table 12, p.141; Table 2.21: p.166; Table 4.11: p.196; Table 5.11: p.228

Interaction between the Mainstream and the Margin

In each case, the contact between the mainstream and the respective 'tribal' group has been going on for a very long time. In southern Africa, the Khoisan peoples were caught between the Bantu-speaking peoples coming southward and the Europeans from overseas penetrating the Continent northward from the Cape peninsula. We lack the detailed history of this spate of migration, but partly it is contained in the rock paintings and folklores of the communities involved. The use of a written language to narrate this history started only after the arrival of Europeans in the post-Vasco da Gama period. Even then, there was hardly any local historian to present the story from within the local society.

In India, the gradual absorption of individual tribes into the caste system via adaptation to what Mandelbaum calls 'civilizational characteristics' (Mandelbaum, 1998: 591) has been known and recorded over a long period. Ancient Hindu scriptures mention tribes who often had a symbiotic relationship with surrounding peasant societies and other communities. According to John Garret's *A Classical Dictionary of India,* both the *Mahabharata* and the

Ramayana mention the Bhils, occupying a territory to the south (Mahabharata) or the east (Ramayana) of the Jamuna River, 'acknowledging or dreading the supremacy of the Kshatriyas' (p.95). The same group was referred to as Nishada in Vedic literature (Bhattacharyya: 1997, 142). There seems to be a continuity of oral (and recorded) history of the Bhil-Rajput contact over time, indicating different stages of their incorporation into the larger social framework. The exploits of Arjuna, the third Pandava, in Manipur (including his romantic involvement with Princess Chitrangada) are well-known episodes of the Mahabharata. This epic also mentions the land of the Nagas, one of whose kings, Ganapati Naga, is cited in the Allahabad inscription of Samudragupta, the most illustrious Gupta emperor (*ibid.* 667). In the *Vishnu Purana*, there are references to the Mundas or Murandas who according to some observers are no other than the Huns. One of the edicts of Asoka, the third emperor of the Maurya dynasty of Magadha tells us that 'the beloved of the gods (meaning King Asoka) even reasons with the forest tribes in his empire, and seeks to reform them.' Some historians would trace the beginning of the process of tribal assimilation in the Gangetic plain even earlier, to sixth century B.C., initiated by the kingdoms of Kosala and Magadha.

Many who have reported on the interaction between the all-India Hindu system and local customs have spoken of the Great Traditions and the Little Traditions. M.N. Srinivas introduced into Indian sociology the concept of Sanskritization as a heuristic tool to throw light on the modus operandi of structural change, involving castes and tribes, in Indian society. A fascinating element in this process is the dispersal, over the ages, of the Rama-Katha (the legend of Rama) through folklores and tribal versions of the story of Rama (Singh & Datta: 1993) – a trend dramatised by the discovery, some years ago, of the Mizo edition of the story.

Probably an important point of difference between India and southern Africa is the presence of historians, social scientists and social critics from within India to record and comment on the process. What is perhaps more significant is the availability of people who are most directly concerned with the process to do this. Not surprisingly, trained anthropologists sponsored by the Anthropological Survey of India have not limited themselves to the study of 'tribes', but have in addition conducted research on non-tribal communities including peasant societies and upper caste Hindu communities. The symbiotic interface between these groups at various stages of development has been the focus of the Survey's research, thus highlighting the long-standing contact between the mainstream and the margin.

In southern Africa, on the other hand, outsiders, i.e. mostly scholars of European and North American origin performed this task. These professional anthropologists studied their target communities *in situ*, following the fieldwork methodology developed by Malinowski and Radcliffe-Brown. The latter even spent some time at the University of Cape Town in South Africa, teaching and training students. Later, research organisations such as the Rhodes-Livingstone Institute in Zambia (then Northern Rhodesia) initiated a series of investigations focused on various tribes in southern Africa. In all these operations, however, there was very little input from African communities, almost nothing from the Khoisan peoples.

In India, the long period of co-existence and co-functioning of the urban sector and peasant societies sustaining the caste system resulted in a kind of integration of the mainstream and different marginalised communities, although they did not occupy equivalent positions. As Mandelbaum says:

> *Although there are great cultural and social differences among the tribal peoples dispersed across India, some preliminary generalizations can be made about them.*
>
> *Among none of these peoples is there the complete dichotomy between tribal culture and civilization which appeared when Europeans first confronted native peoples in the Americas, Africa, and Oceania. Even the most remote and isolated tribal groups in India has certain cultural traits in common with jati people, as for example in the nature of*

purity and pollution, in the worship of local spirits, and in kinship practices. (Mandelbaum, 1998:575-76)

Khoisan Policy and the Status of the Khoisan

This essay deals mainly with Khoisan policies in southern Africa and 'tribal' policies in India. The word 'policy' stands for a consciously formulated course of action with regard to a specific phenomenon or issue, usually proposed by the decision-makers – the government and/or other administrative authorities at various levels. This is at the formal and manifest level. I would like to widen this perspective to include the major strategies of the society to address the same phenomenon. This of course includes the proclaimed 'policy' of the government, but additionally covers such items as the dominant attitudes in society with regard to the issue, often compressed into stereotypes, and the unwritten dos and don'ts governing inter-group relations. In the colonial situation, this embraced, additionally, the beliefs and practices of the actors who may not have formed part of the local society.

Since long, the Khoisan, and especially the San have evoked considerable interest at home and abroad – first as a anthropological singularity surrounded by Bantu-speaking black communities of a less diluted 'Negroid' stock, and English- and Afrikaans-speaking whites. To this was added their linguistic distinctiveness, due to the surfeit of 'click' sounds in their speeches, among other things.

In the early nineteenth century, popular construction of race added a new dimension to Bushman studies, symbolising a mixture of ethnicity and sex, gauged in terms particularly of the sizes of certain parts of Khoisan bodies, and an amalgam of pseudo-science and what bordered on voyeuristic pleasure.

Scientifically it may not be wise to pinpoint an individual for a major historical watershed, but the notorious Saartjie Baartman episode epitomized contemporary Western conceptualisation of Khoisan identity. If to the uninitiated it promised erotic exotica, to the more 'scientifically' disposed, it served as a living 'missing link'. Designated as the 'Hottentot Venus', Saartjie Baartmam was 'acquired' by a certain Alexander Dunlop from the Eastern Cape and was exhibited as a sex symbol in private parties of the high and mighty in Europe, to be subsequently shown in public theatres. Saartjie Baartman was to be followed by others, one of whom was displayed in Banyoles Museum in Spain as 'El Negro' (The Bushman) and caused a public storm some time back because of its ideological overtones.

Towards the close of the 19th century, a series of academic expeditions took hundreds of photographs and moulds of Khoisan bodies many of which survive in museum collections and archives in South Africa and Europe. The 'civilized' man's concern for preserving a lasting record of the vanishing type generated a record harvest. San, says Gordon, are 'one of the most heavily scientifically commoditized human groupings in the academic endeavour' (Gordon, 1990:1; quoted by White, 1955:3). To this, someone added: '...the economic metaphor invoked here holds literally in the field of popular cultural consumption as well', what with the demand for San artifacts, real or replica (White, 1995:3).

Hardly anything remained of the San that was not placed under the 'scientific' scrutiny of the visiting academic for the proclaimed advancement of science and as contribution to his/her career advancement – language, myths, material culture, social structure, world view, and even blood, saliva, and urine in exchange for a little tobacco and European drink. This was indeed a paltry price demanded by the 'noble savage' for scientific advancement of humanity that benefited him but little!

Such specific projects did not detract from the overall thrust of Bushman studies. An important cause of disagreement between independent governments of some of the southern African countries and foreign researchers, mainly white with some Japanese participation, centred on the issue of what to do with the San. Should they be kept as museum pieces as exemplified later by the Kagga Kamma 'experiment' or should they be encouraged or even persuaded to join the mainstream as part of the wider development process, keeping their land and culture? The latter approach is illustrated by what John Hardbattle stood for in Botswana and what the Griqua National Conference currently aims at in South Africa. In parenthesis, it may be noted that mostly this strategy has found favour in India too, except that a heated, but inconclusive, debate rages about what is happening to some of the most 'primitive' and dying communities in the subcontinent such as the Jarwa whose desperate condition has been mentioned later.

An idea that sustained the 'museum piece' thesis in southern Africa was the early belief that the San are genetically different from other ethnic types (Sanders, 1995:8). This point alone explains why so much effort was spent on research in physical or biological anthropology of the San. A variation on this theme is summed up in the 'hybridization' hypothesis held by many in positions of authority to mean that the San are genetically distant from the rest of humanity and that they are incapable of interbreeding with others. That there is little scientific value in this position was demonstrated through Tom Hardbattle's marriage with a Nharo (a branch of the San) woman, the mother of John Hardbattle.

However, even if the idea of genetical isolation of the San is rejected, the so-called civilisational angle continued to dominate Western research circles. The San were taken as the missing link in the evolutionary process. They were the Stone Age remnants of human past. They formed the counterpoint of the West – the evocative evolutionary 'others', the alter-ego, and the counterfoil to the image of Western modernity. Therefore, the precious heritage of the Khoisan of the present day is to be documented and preserved for the future.

Inevitably, with the passage of time and the victorious march of capitalism worldwide, the scientific interest merged with the commercial. Meanwhile, piqued by curiosity, the tourist industry flourished. Pippa Skotness ("An Obsession for Khoisan Genitalia" in *Mail and Guardian*, February 16-22, 1996), Senior Lecturer in Fine Arts at the University of Cape Town, reports that by the middle of the 19th Century, Khoisan bodies were considered so extraordinary that thousands of Europeans were prepared to pay for seeing them in southern Africa or the West.

A comment made by Jaume *et al.* although made with reference to the stuffed body of a San male preserved in the Catalan museum of Banyoles in Spain, sums up the manner in which Western interest in San ethnography has evolved and how, through this evolution, science has rubbed shoulders with less noble preoccupations. One could have added that in all these operations pseudo-science has masqueraded as science.

> *Initially, the centre of funerary ritual, it (the body of El-Negro) then became a scientific curiosity framed in a colonial context. Once in Europe, it became a commercial object, being traded between various collectors, and on the death of Darder, it became a token of benefaction towards the town of Banyoles. Today it has become a symbol of racism and is seen by some sectors of the Banyoles community to express their dissatisfaction with recent black immigration (into Spain). (Jaume, 1993: 117)*

Khoisan historiography is additionally distinctive because it internationalised scientific research focused on these communities by generating an intense competition among academics of various nationalities. Insofar as a large section, if not a majority, of the Khoisan peoples live in Botswana which was a British protectorate before 1966 and a poor undeveloped country for more than a decade after Independence, the pressure on this country was marked.

Can we imagine how the French would have reacted if the Chinese set up an institute of Corsican Studies in Beijing and lectured the French on the type of research that should be undertaken on Corsican society or rendered unsolicited advice on the legal status of the Corsicans in mainland France? Yet a situation similar to this was emerging about research on the San population of Botswana (known as the Basarwa in the country) before Botswana's independence. In 1956, a number of academics from the University of Witwatersrand and some other institutions of

South Africa created the Kalahari Research Committee (KRC) whose members were drawn almost exclusively from the white South African community.

A more aggressive and potentially interventionist, posture was taken by the Coordinating Committee for Bushman Studies, a forum of academics based in the West, at a meeting held at the University of London in October 1960. A matter of particular relevance to our present purpose was a gathering, which argued that the interests of the San should be 'represented' while drafting the new constitution of the Bechuanaland Protectorate.

A comparable sentiment was expressed to a heightened degree by the Anti-Slavery Society that had been showing interest in the fate of the peoples of colonies. The Society's annual report for the year ending on 31st March 1966 said, with an exemplary show of self-righteousness, if the Society did not protect the rights of the Khoisan, 'nobody else in the world will be in the slightest degree interested'! Whereas the desperate condition of the Khoisan is not a matter of dispute, one wonders why the 'conscience' of researchers and certain 'do-gooders' of the West was dormant so long and why it was raised with such fervour just on the eve of political liberation in southern Africa.

In the circumstances, the independent government of Botswana decided that Khoisan studies including research needed to be firmly located within the framework of the nation's sovereignty. With this end in view, the Government passed the Anthropological Research Act in 1967 to formalise national control over both monitoring research on the Khoisan and the direction of the developmental process relating to the Khoisan.

The feeling that the Khoisan were being 'over-researched' was not restricted to Botswana. At the London University meeting, mentioned above, somebody felt the need for creating a society for protecting the Khoisan in Botswana from 'indiscriminate investigation'. Several years later, the Bushman Settlement Officer of the Government of Botswana reported that some researchers over-stressed the exotic life style of the Khoisan, forgetting their needs as citizens of a modern state.

Understandably, the number of investigations was not the main issue here. It might have been the prospect of what bridge players call the 'pre-emptive bid' in certain foreign quarters to control research in an important sector of southern African society that was causing concern. It may be wrong to deny that some of the actors in this bizarre scenario had legitimate professional interest plus a dash of humanitarianism in the research in question. However, the 'take-over' bid was at times accompanied by less noble sentiments. In one of the meetings attended by Western researchers, someone even spoke of the British efforts 'to corner the Bushman market'. This was indeed a stark reminder of the ease with which the rat-race lingo of the marketplace can invade even the sacred precincts of the ivory tower!

In all this academic and ideological hullabaloo, potentially the most directly concerned contributor is conspicuously missing – the Khoisan himself. Outside researchers have been recording, translating and interpreting their oral traditions recited by clan elders. But how do the Khoisan themselves perceive the arrival among others, of the Bakgalagari, the Batswana, the Batawana, the Baherero – all Bantu-speaking black communities – and the Afrikaner? Do we know what their view is of the impact of a host of other developments such as the rinderpest epidemic of the 1890s, the drought of the 1930s, the relentless penetration of the capitalist mode of production into their territory including the expansion of trade, commercial agriculture, tourism, and employment in the formal sector? It is not being suggested that only Khoisan can write Khoisan history; but it is time there was general agreement that unless they do so, a critical dimension will be missing from their historiography. Furthermore, central to the questions raised above is the Khoisan self-image: the manner in which they define their own social identity in relation to other ethnic communities of southern Africa.

In the recent past, some efforts have been made to stimulate Khoisan contribution to the debate. A conservative trend that fails to challenge the dominant stereotype of the Khoisan widely prevalent in the white community, is represented by David Kruiper, leader of a small group of 'traditional' San hunter-gatherers at Kagga Kamma Nature Reserve in the Northern Cape Province of South Africa. Three white wine merchants who collected about thirty San hunter-gatherers created this Reserve and have been 'displaying' the San residents to curious visitors. Kruiper affirmed, publicly and candidly, his and his followers' representation as the last relic of the earliest humanity.

> *I am an animal of nature. I want people to see me and know who I am. The only way our tradition and way of life can survive is to live in the memory of the people who see me.* (Quoted by White, 1995:17)

Kruiper's world vision is characterised by the rejection of modern innovations, both technological and social, a stress on the need to live in close communion with nature, a belief in the sanctity of traditions, a strong impulse to keep his own language, culture and way of life, and last but not least, an urge to preserve genetic purity. Kruiper highlights the last point by contrasting the San with the 'basters'. These are South Africans of mixed racial origin and are popularly referred to in English as 'bastards', although in terms of the Population Registration Act of 1950, they have been officially classified as 'coloureds'. Kruiper could not have been more specific.

> *The largest (sic) difference between a Bushman and a Baster (sic)is that a Bushman wants to keep his Bushman tradition, but not a Baster. He just wants to be a Whiteman...I have my own language...but where is the Baster language?* (White, 1995: 19)

We do not know how representative Kruiper's worldview is among Khoisan communities in southern Africa. But certainly there are alternative attempts at coming to grips with the present and using a reconstruction of the past as legitimising the actions currently initiated.

John Hardbattle, son of a British immigrant farmer and a

Nharo mother, set up in his life time an organization called The First People of the Kalahari to represent the Nharo, the T/aakwe, the G//anakwe, the G/wikwe and the #Au//ae of Botswana. Its objectives are (1) to work for the land rights of the people concerned, (2) the 'invigoration' of the culture, (3) the dissemination of information, and (4) contacting and strengthening links with other first peoples. The ultimate goal is to 'break through the apathy imposed on us through the loss of our ancestral lands, our rights to water, the gathering of peoples in settlements, the dependency of living off the drought relief' (Hardbattle, 1993: 141). Under his leadership, The First People of the Kalahari attended for the first time a national meeting entitled the Botswana Society Workshop for Sustainable Development in Gaborone in 1992. Thereafter, a delegation of the First People of the Kalahari met with Botswana government leaders to discuss their problems. Unfortunately, the meeting proved abortive. Still later, Hardbattle led a delegation to some European countries and to the United Nations. Shortly afterwards he died, leaving a society shorn of leadership.

Comparable moves were being initiated elsewhere. In South Africa, the Griqua National Conference (GNC) was set up as early as 1914 to speak for the Griqua community and to build a collective identity on the reconstruction of the past. The Griqua trace descent from one Adam Kok I who led his Khoi followers to what now is the Northern Cape Province of South Africa, south of the Orange River. Others, including some of mixed stock, joined them later. Today most Griqua speak Afrikaans, the mother tongue of the Afrikaners, but the original Griqua language is still alive. In fact, Kate Cloete, Secretary of GNC, insists that the language should receive constitutional recognition. Parenthetically, the new constitution of South Africa has declared eleven languages as official, none of which is of Khoisan stock.

In December 1995, the GNC, through a memorandum to President Mandela, asked for the recognition of the Griqua community as an 'indigenous or First Nation of South Africa' together with their land entitlement. In a separate move, the GNC addressed to the French embassy in Pretoria calling for the return of Saartjie Baartman's remains – her brain, skeleton, and genitals, preserved in a back room at the Museé de l'Homme in Paris. Ironically, Baartman was born in 1789 when the French Revolution started. The Revolution inspired the Declaration of the Rights of Man that is mentioned in the GNC submission, in vindication of Griqua rights. In 1995, The GNC was represented at the UN working group for indigenous people

The struggle of the Griqua, like that of other Khoisan peoples, for the defence of their rights and for the establishment of their identity has not been easy; but Cloete's enthusiasm is contagious. The Griqua have adopted a desert plant called the *kanniedood* (meaning 'cannot die') as their emblem. 'We are a kanniedood people', says Cloete.

The debate about the objective(s), direction and implementation of an appropriate strategy for tribal administration for development is a kind of ideological struggle, although many mundane considerations hide it effectively. In southern Africa, we have referred above to the manner in which the target groups have sought to create a space for themselves in this palaver and how their perception and definition of the situation in which they find themselves have contributed to the agenda of the debate. A modern researcher without evolutionary pretensions may not care to test the 'peadomorphic' hypothesis of Tobias to explain why the San people have what some whites thought 'child-like' features, and push them to an earlier evolutionary stage. Today, fifty years later, questions of social development are more pertinent and the buzzwords are not just per capita income and productivity, but education, health, and the quality of life. The thrusts of research and ancillary studies have changed largely because new actors have appeared on the stage with fresh ideological orientations and articulations. The time will soon come when Khoisan academics and ideologues will offer their own perspective(s), probably generating appropriate paradigmatic shifts in South African historiography.

It is relevant to stress here that the debate at the national level is about power and self-determination. The Botswana story about the control over research on probably the largest concentration of Khoisan population shows, clearly, that decolonization is not merely political. In fact, tracing the gradual unfolding of the debate, we can see that manufacturing knowledge of the past and of the present, coupled with the probe for a worthwhile stratagem for the future, is another dimension of the process of power generation. The decision makers of a country can ignore this conclusion only at their peril, especially when voices so long suppressed are joining in the battle, increasingly on their own terms.

The near extinction of the San in South Africa has rendered a discussion of their position irrelevant. Today neither the San nor the Khoi occupy any compact territory in South Africa that can be called their habitat. In the inter-War period, there was some talk of creating a settlement or reserve for the San of Botswana, South Africa and South West Africa (now Namibia). Yet, even in the heyday of apartheid, when Bantustans or so-called homelands for non-whites were being set up [(5)], there was no serious proposal for creating a reserve exclusively for the Khoisan of South Africa. The new constitution of the country recognises eleven languages as official [(6)], but the list does not include a Khoisan language. However, the South African Government has set up the Pan South African Language Board (PaNSALB) to initiate research for promoting the development of the Khoisan languages. Under the Board, the Khoi and San National Language bodies were created in 1999 to launch appropriate programmes. To address sensitive issues such as portrayal of Khoisan in museums as showpieces, the South African Heritage Resources Agency (SAHRA) has been launched. Of some significance is the inclusion of a Khoisan saying in the Coat of Arms of the country.[(7)]

In Botswana, Section 14(3) C of the Constitution provides for 'the imposition of restriction on the entry into or residence within defined areas of Botswana of persons who are not Bushmen to the extent that such restrictions are reasonably required for the protection or well-being of Bushmen.' Yet the situation is not without an element of ambiguity insofar as the Government generally acts on the opinion of the Attorney-General's Chambers that the San (the local term being the 'Basarwa') have no rights of any kind to land, except for hunting. This view is offered on the assumption that the San 'have always been true nomads.' (Quoted by Mogwe, 1992: 5)

In the entire region, the position of the Khoisan is the least discriminatory in Namibia. Already, the government of Namibia (formerly the colony of South West Africa) has designated a region, NyaeNyae, as 'Bushmanland'. Although Namibia is a unitary state, the local administration of this district enjoys certain powers that make it possible for them to address the problems of the Khoisan.

Tribal Policy and Administration in British India

Tribal administration in southern Africa can now be compared and contrasted with what has been happening in South Asia, starting with the beginning of British rule in India. With the introduction of the British administration coupled with the penetration of the capitalist mode of production and Christian missionary bodies, the need was felt for a coherent policy to deal with non-Hindu and non-Moslem Indians. The immediate reason for intervention was the near-revolt of the Paharia people of the Rajmahal Hills on the western fringe of Bengal. Although Hindu *zamindars* were the immediate target of the Paharia protest, it had implications for the recently established administration of the East India Company. In 1782, the Rajmahal Hills were separated from the areas directly administered by the Company and were placed under a Hill Assembly that was authorised to make rules for the administration of the segregated area. In 1833, certain areas of Chotanagpur were declared as non-regulated areas where outsiders were not allowed to acquire land. However, this did not solve the problem of exploitation of the marginalised communities. In 1855, the Santal revolt broke out in an adjacent region.

The situation did not materially change after the introduction of direct British rule in the wake of the 1857 mutiny. In the 1860s through the 1870s, measures sanctioning the establishment of specially administered non-regulation areas were extended to various regions. The Inner Line Regulation of 1873 was aimed at bringing under stringent control the commercial relations of members of the mainstream with the marginalised communities of the north-eastern regions. The Government of India Act, 1919 formalised variations on the theme by creating 'partially excluded' and 'wholly excluded' areas. Simultaneously, the interface between the mainstream and the margin was diversified by introducing three systems of representation. Some excluded areas were given the right of representation in the central and provincial legislatures. Others enjoyed the right of representation by proxy because their 'representatives' were nominated. Some other excluded areas had no right of representation in provincial and central legislatures. Minor changes in these provisions took place in the Government of India Act of 1935. One of these resulted in the appointment of tribal enquiry committees in several provinces, e.g. Bihar, Bombay, Madras and Orissa. These committees functioned with reference to partially excluded areas in which popularly elected ministries (of the mainstream) enjoyed some limited powers. In time, this trend might have generated a fruitful interaction between the mainstream and the representatives of the margins, even if mediated by colonial administration. However, the outbreak of World War II aborted the prospect.

The tribal policy of British India was essentially negative; it did not look forward to the emergence of a united India embracing communities with different languages, religions, social systems, and cultures. It did not address the central issue of development in a situation like this: What kind of development are we thinking of for the marginalised communities and at what price? In effect, the thrust of the British Indian policy was to maintain the status quo, as long as it helped the penetration of capitalism in the interior and left Pax Britannica undisturbed.

Tribal Policy and Administration in India since Independence

After independence, have we really broken through the straitjacket of conventional thinking? Let us note that there has never been an official tribal policy as such. At one stage, there was some discussion of the strategy of Verrier Elwin encapsulated in the National Park thesis. Let us recall that Elwin's plan advocated complete withdrawal from tribal areas, leaving the process of development to the people concerned.

Later, there was some talk about Nehru's Panchsheel, the main principles of which may thus be summed up.

1. Nothing is to be imposed on tribal communities. People should be encouraged to develop along the lines of their own genius.
2. Full respect should be extended to tribal rights in land and forests.
3. For taking care of administration and development, a local team of officers should be built up. The tendency to inject too many outsiders should be checked.
4. The task of administration and development should be carried out through social and cultural institutions of the community. Over-administration of tribal areas should be avoided.
5. Development should be assessed not by statistics or the amount of money spent. The touchstone of progress will be the quality of human character that is evolved.

Panchsheel has the typical merits and demerits of a policy that is couched in general terms. No one can find fault with the principles it spells out. The problem lies with their application and interpretation. Clearly, it is not easy to express in concrete terms what is meant by such phrases as 'too many outsiders' (point 3), 'over-administration' (point 4), and 'the quality of human character' (point 5). Furthermore, whereas generally nothing should be imposed upon tribal communities, we wonder if they can be entirely isolated from developments taking place elsewhere in the country in the implementation of which they had any say. Panchsheels's denunciation of money spent on development as a yardstick to gauge progress is well taken. Nevertheless, the solution is not to project 'the quality of human life' as the goal, without operationalising the phrase. Especially when a 'policy statement' ends with a call to develop 'the quality of human character', it surely paves the way for an inordinate palaver!

Perhaps as a backlash to the National Park thesis and the Panchsheel doctrine, people like eminent sociologist G.S. Ghurye argued in favour of full assimilation of tribal communities into the mainstream. The debate on this issue is still unresolved; meanwhile embarrassing reports of sufferings of marginalised groups come to the surface in the national press and other forums at regular intervals. The problem is particularly acute for tribes such as the Jarwa in the Andaman and Nicober Islands whose desperate condition was highlighted by the Society for Andaman and Nicobar Ecology (SANE) in April 2004.

Interestingly, even if the basic strategy of 'tribal administration' is yet uncertain, piecemeal efforts have been made to satisfy the aspirations of the organised sections on the margins. Thus, the Constitution of India specifies several categories of people who have been granted special privileges. The two most important of these are the Scheduled Castes and the Scheduled Tribes. The position extended to the first group goes back to 1932 when the Communal Award created especially reserved constituencies for the 'Depressed Classes' – an earlier appellation in British-Indian parlance for the Scheduled Castes.

The Scheduled Tribes : Special Treatment in the Constitution

In the post-independence period, a number of constitutional

measures have been adopted making way for special treatment to be meted out to the Scheduled Tribes. Some of these are applicable, *mutatis mutandis*, to the Scheduled Castes as well. There are, in addition, certain provisions that are specific to the Scheduled Castes, e.g., the prohibition of 'untouchability' (Article 17).

Articles

15 (1) & (2)	Prevention of discrimination on grounds of religion, race, caste, sex or place of birth with regard to access to public places and places of public resort maintained wholly or partially out of state funds or dedicated to the use of general public
15 (4)	Empowering the State to reserve seats in the public educational institutions and to make other special provisions such as providing housing accommodation for Scheduled Castes and Scheduled Tribes and any socially and educationally backward classes of citizens
16	Permitting the State to make reservations for backward classes in public services in case of inadequate representations
19 (5)	Curtailment by law in the interests of any Scheduled Tribes of general rights of all citizens to move freely, settle in, and acquire property
23	Prohibition of traffic in human beings and forced labour
29 (2)	Forbidding of any denial of admission to educational institutions maintained by State or receiving grant out of State funds
46	Promotion of the educational and economic interests of Scheduled Castes and Scheduled Tribes and other weaker sections, and their protection from social injustice and all forms of exploitation

164	In Bihar, Madhya Pradesh and Orissa, appointment of a minister in charge of tribal welfare who may additionally be in charge of the Scheduled Castes and backward classes
244 & 5th Schedule	Administration of Scheduled Castes and Scheduled Tribes in States other than Assam
244 6th Schedule	Administration of the tribal areas in the State of Assam
330	Reservation of seats for Scheduled Castes and Scheduled Tribes in the Lok Sabha (lower house of the Indian Parliament)
332	Reservation of seats for Scheduled Castes and Scheduled Tribes in the Legislative Assemblies of the States
335	Requiring the State to consider claims of Scheduled Castes and Scheduled Tribes in the making of appointments to public services
338	Appointment of a Special Officer for Scheduled Castes and Scheduled Tribes. The Special Officer's post under this Article was later replaced by the National Commission for Scheduled Castes and Scheduled Tribes under the 65th Amendment
342	Specification of Scheduled Tribes

Evaluation of Tribal Reservation in India

Currently out of the 543 seats of the Lok Sabha (lower house of the Indian Parliament), 41 are reserved for the Scheduled Tribes. In the Legislative Assemblies of the States, 1081 seats out of a total of 4091 seats are reserved for the Scheduled Castes and the Scheduled Tribes.

In the employment sector, there are reserved posts for the Scheduled Castes, the Scheduled Tribes, and other backward classes. In addition, there is provision for reservation for the physically handicapped and ex-servicemen in certain categories of posts. The percentages of reservation for the Scheduled Castes, the Scheduled Tribes and Other Backward Classes in direct recruitment by open competition are 15%, 7½%, and 27% respectively. Direct recruitment by open competition in this context means recruitment on an all-India basis via the Union Public Service Commission, Staff Selection Commission or any other appointing authority through written examination or by interview or both. In direct recruitment on an all-India basis by a method other than open competition, the corresponding sizes of reservation for the Scheduled Castes, the Scheduled Tribes, and Other Backward Classes are $16^2/_3$%, 7½%, and 27% respectively. In promotion, the proportions of reservation for the Scheduled Castes and the Scheduled Tribes are 15% and 7½% respectively, provided the quantum of direct recruitment does not go beyond 75%.

Table 4.2: *Representation of Scheduled Castes and Scheduled Tribes in Central Government Services (In percentages; As on 1 January 1995)*

Service categories	*Scheduled Castes*	*Scheduled Tribes*
Group A (top layer)	10.15	2.89
Group B	12.67	2.68
Group C	16.15	5.69
Group D (lowest layer)	21.26	6.48
Sub-total (excluding *safai karmachari* or cleaners)	17.43	5.78
Total (including *safai karmachari* or cleaners)	18.71	5.83

Source: Government of India: Ministry of Information & Broadcasting, *India 1998: a Reference Manual.* New Delhi, 1998. P. 198

It is agreed that the reservation under Art. 16(4) should not, as a rule, exceed 50% of vacancies arising in a year, but may be extended in extraordinary circumstances. Taking advantage of this provision, the Tamil Nadu Government enacted the Tamil Nadu

Reservation Act (45 of 1994) which authorised the Tamil Nadu Government to make reservation covering up to 69% of the available positions (18% Scheduled Castes, 1% Scheduled Tribes, 50% Other Backward Classes). The Act was brought within the purview of the Ninth Schedule to the Constitution so that it could be shielded from judicial review.

At the time of the drafting of the constitution, reservation for the Scheduled Castes and the Scheduled Tribes in the Parliament and State Legislative Assemblies was generally accepted as a follow-up measure of the 1932 Communal Award. However, this was envisaged for a period of ten years only. Since then the application of Art. 330 (1) has been extended five times, after every ten years, through constitutional amendment. In terms of the latest constitutional amendment, reservation of seats for these groups will come to an end on 26 January 2010, unless it is renewed again.

Along with reservation of seats in the Parliament and State legislative Assemblies, the Scheduled Castes and the Scheduled Tribes have been enjoying some privileges in matters relating to employment and access to educational institutions. With effect from the 1990s, reservation in employment and educational institutions was extended additionally to the so-called Other Backward Classes (OBCs) thereby complicating an already complex situation.

A basic difficulty of the reservation issue as it emerges from the Indian case relates to its lack of conceptual clarity. This has been due to an uncritical use of several terms – all supposed to subsume marginality labelled as 'backwardness', of different shades and types. The fathers of the constitution made elaborate provisions for the Scheduled Castes and the Scheduled Tribes, apart from ensuring representation for the Anglo-Indians in the Parliament. They additionally stressed the need for affirmative action in favour of the 'socially and educationally backward classes' [Art. 15 (4) and Art. 340], the 'weaker sections of the people' [Art.46], and the 'backward classes' [Art.16 (4)]. No attempt was made to subject these terms to a precise and rigorous definition in the constitution – a situation that has led to confusion. As a result, there has been an intermittent debate regarding the actual overlap between caste, tribe and class as indicators of social inequity.

A corollary of this point takes us to the neglect of inner contradictions, i. e. of class formation that have been developing over the years within a backward caste or tribe. This is surprising in view of the repeated allegations made in the mass media and elsewhere that the special privileges granted to the Scheduled Castes and the Scheduled Tribes are being cornered by a small, but already well-to-do and well-entrenched, section of the target group, thus preventing the percolation of the benefits of the system down to those who really need them. The provision for the 'creamy layer'(7) among Other Backward Classes, a kind of de-marginalisation of certain categories of persons, may at best be regarded as a clumsy attempt to marry the caste and the class dimensions. It is necessary to note that there is no provision for establishing a creamy layer within a tribe.

Some observers believe that the establishment of a separate category of the so-called 'Other Backward Classes' (not 'castes'!) was a strategy to create an electoral space for the authors of this move. Predictably, this development has opened a veritable Pandora's Box. In many parts of the country, the dominant peasant castes, e.g. the Yadav, the Kurmi, the Reddy, the Kamma, the Vokkaliga, the Jat, etc. have lobbied and indeed successfully agitated for the backward class status. This development seems to be giving a new lease of life to caste consciousness and inter-caste tension, instead of putting an end to them. Is there any reason why a similar situation will not emerge among the Scheduled Tribes? Indeed, the creation of a category of 'Primitive Tribal Groups' (PTGs) may point to this direction.

Beyond the size of reservation, looms the issue of justifying the very idea of reservation. Reservation of legislative representation, jobs, and admission to educational and vocational institutions on a quota basis is a distinctively Indian experiment. Of course, there have been official attempts in other countries to provide help to disadvantaged communities. In the USA, for instance, the principle of affirmative action defined as 'a formal effort to provide increased employment opportunities for women and ethnic minorities to overcome past patterns of discrimination' has been in vogue. The Equal Employment Opportunity Act of 1972 enjoined various public authorities 'to initiate plans to increase the proportions of their female and minority employees until they matched the proportions existing in the available labour market.' Although the application of the Act created a lot of confusion and was challenged at different times, the Clinton administration strongly defended the principle of affirmative action, stressing at the same time that it is to be applied with caution.

The concept of 'affirmative action', 'positive discrimination', and 'protective discrimination' (or any of its variants) is closely linked to two associated, but competing, notions: equality of opportunity and equality of results. There is little controversy about the rationale of the equality of opportunity. However, the principle of equality of results has promoted a heated debate. Its exponents argue that simply abolishing discriminatory practices is not enough because it cannot be expected to achieve equality in a society permeated by inequality. Its opponents charge, with equal vehemence, that the principle serves to put people in places based on their affiliation to a protected group (ascription) and without regard to individual merit (achievement).

Finally, the whole system of reservations points to a departure from the principle of making the individual the central focus of development. In this latter dispensation, compensatory measures for the Scheduled Castes and the Scheduled Tribes can be justified at best as exceptional and for a limited period only.

The pull of the Mandal Commission[(9)] seems currently to be stronger than this alternative ideal. Some sociologists (e.g. Yogendra Singh, 1997: 218-19) argue that the forces unleashed by the Mandal Commission are functional to the Indian polity because they have 'contributed to the rapid integration of the backward classes in

Indian society.' For the same reason, special treatment for the Scheduled Tribes based on an elaborate system of reservation can arguably be functional to the stability of Indian society. Only a thorough cost-benefit analysis will reveal the extent to which this is the case, the nature of integration that is supposed to be taking place, and the cost at which this is being realised.

Conclusion

The experiences of southern Africa and India in dealing with special problems of 'backwardness', crystallized in the situations in which marginalised ethnic communities find themselves, are fascinating to compare. An account of this is indicative of differences in the historical background of the two regions, their exposure to and familiarity with democratic traditions, and the strategies adopted by the authorities in the two regions to address the problem of establishing a more harmonious interface between the mainstream and the margins.

The history of the contact between Khoisan peoples and both the whites and Bantu-speakers in southern Africa is just about five hundred years old, at least in areas south of the Orange River. By contrast, the mainstream of Indian society has had contact with tribal communities since several centuries before the beginning of the Christian era. References have been made above to the gradual assimilation of tribal groups in the Gangetic plain within the kingdoms of Kosala and Magadha. This happened in the sixth century B.C. There is reason to believe that the process continued over time. About two hundred years later, King Asoka's edicts suggest that the political establishment of the mainstream was attempting to reach a kind of *modus vivendi* with various tribal groups. This process has not always led to assimilation of the marginalised groups into the mainstream; sometimes the two parties co-existed in contrast. Mandelbaum gives an illuminating illustration. 'The Konds of Baderi village have lived within two miles of an Oriya caste village for perhaps as many as eight centuries and have remained tribal Konds.' (1998: 585) Certain other groups have remained isolated and some of them still live in isolation from the mainstream. Yet, overall, the picture is one of a steady process of contact and interaction, spread over thousands of years, literally, often leading to assimilation of one sort or another.

The treatment meted out to marginalised tribes by the mainstream in each region speaks of harassment, bias and discrimination. Members of both sides reciprocally hold stereotypes, often uncomplimentary. Yet, India was spared of the extreme form of racial oppression and humiliation that the marginalised groups in southern Africa experienced. Moreover, marginalised Indians were not subjected to the indignities of being exhibited like performing animals in Europe. It is against this background that the investigations in southern Africa inspired by wild pseudo-scientific premises, e.g. the 'paedomorphic' hypothesis and the hybridisation theory should be evaluated.

Thus, history has been of help to India in bringing the mainstream and the margin together, although not necessarily on equivalent terms. The process of contact and interaction has additionally been helped by India's longer exposure to political and administrative democracy, when compared to southern Africa. The democratic process in India formally extended legal and constitutional rights to the marginalised tribal groups more than half a century before. This did not come about simply as an imposition from above. There was widespread and long-drawn-out public debate centring on various demands voiced by certain marginalised groups. Hard bargains were negotiated in the inter-War period involving specific caste groups and especially the Dalits. One of the most famous of these culminated in the Communal Award of Puna (later renamed Pune) in 1932. Many tribal groups were still out of bounds for the mainstream national movements because of the application of the policy of 'excluded' and 'partially excluded areas' and of 'the Inner Line Policy' that sought to control entry of other Indians into tribal territories. Nevertheless, there was expectation that all tribes including those who were isolated fully or partly would have access to what the Dalits got. By contrast, political democracy made its debut in southern Africa only in the late 1960s, with the decolonisation of Botswana, Lesotho and Swaziland. Zimbabwe (then Rhodesia) had to wait for more than a decade to shake off colonial rule, while South Africa saw the establishment of a fully democratic government only in 1994.

In both cases, the governments aided by NGOs have attempted integration of marginalised tribal groups and the mainstream through diverse ways. Two of these deserve special mention: (1) launching projects seeking to benefit the marginalised groups directly, and (2) establishing appropriate legal and constitutional agencies aimed at empowering and developing them.

In India, projects seeking to benefit the Scheduled Tribes and other marginalised groups include various educational schemes, the Tribal Sub-Plans (TSPs), the Integrated Tribal Development Projects (ITDPs), the Modified Area Development Project (MADA), Tribal Cooperative Marketing Development, Village Grain Banks, and Grants-in-Aid for Minor Forest Produce Operations. Likewise, in southern Africa, projects aiming at improving education, agriculture, land use, and health facilities affecting marginalised groups have been in operation. An appropriate example is the Botswana Government's Remote Area Development (RAD) Programme, which starting in 1974 sought to integrate the San people into the mainstream through, among other things, large-scale rehabilitation settlements. A full evaluation of these attempts is not possible in the short space available here. Moreover, projects of this nature can at best be palliative. They do not address the basic issues surrounding the absence of development on the margin.

Perhaps the most important point of difference between the two cases is the elaborate constitutional and legal structures created in India for the protection and development of marginalised communities. A short account of these has been provided above. The core of the structures is the system of reservation, guaranteed constitutionally to marginalised communities – in political representation, jobs, and admission to educational institutions.

The wisdom of this policy, dubbed by some critics as 'competitive backwardness', has been questioned, especially in view of its snowball effect through the extension to other communities of the privileges granted originally to the Scheduled Castes and the Scheduled Tribes.

Today, tribal administration in India is to be described and understood as part of a grand structure in which communities other than tribes such as castes traditionally occupying lower positions in the purity-pollution hierarchy, Anglo-Indians, and middle level castes constitutionally designated as 'Other Backward Classes' also figure.

Ironically, with all these elaborate measures, India can hardly claim greater success than southern Africa in finding a convincing answer to the questions: Whose development? What kind of development? How should it be measured? How should the target group be involved in the process? These questions may not seem very relevant when some success has been achieved in incorporating tribal groups into the political and administrative system of the mainstream of the country. However, they come dramatically to the fore when we consider the cases of small-scale and isolated tribes such as the Jarwa, the Great Andamanese, the Onge and the Sentinelese of the Andaman and Nicober Islands and some other tribes like the Chenchu on the mainland. Over the centuries, these peoples have been declining in number so much that they are now in danger of becoming altogether extinct. [10]

The cross-cultural comparison constituting the main thrust of the present paper is particularly relevant in this context, especially in the light of the lively debate over the notion of poverty in contrast with life at a lower level of subsistence among San communities in southern Africa and similarly placed communities in India. Many of the world's most technically backward peoples have few material possessions, but that does not necessarily make them 'poor' as the term is understood today. They do not have unemployment; nor do they suffer from malnutrition and certain diseases that are prevalent in industrial societies. Modern-day poverty, to be found in the midst of plenty, is a label denoting a certain socio-economic status. Such a stamp is branded on the present-day Khoisan in southern Africa and to tribes such as the Jarwa in India as they exist today.

The controversy about the trunk road in the Andaman Islands cutting through the Jarwa reserved territory symbolises India's predicament. However, Jarwas do not constitute an exceptional case. Are not there many other trunk roads, literally and symbolically, in tribal territories occupied by similar communities and built by insensitive representatives of mainstream groups in southern Africa, India and indeed throughout the 'civilised' world? The irony is that to many unimaginative and pretentious administrators, these trunk roads are sure signs of progress.

A related point that comes out of the flurry of statistics suggests that development should not be, indeed can never be, dissociated from self-determination and empowerment. Development figures relating to constituent states of India and the tribes living there are better where previously marginalised groups have been empowered locally, e.g. most northeastern states of India. On the other hand, in states where, not being in a majority, the marginalised groups do not wield power, their situation leaves much to be desired. The condition of Scheduled Tribes in states dominated by mainstream groups is worse than their condition in states such as Manipur, Meghalaya, Nagaland, and Mizoram as judged by several development indicators. The cases of Chattisgarh and Jharkhand have not been considered here because they attained statehood only recently. India's *National Human Development Report 2001* [Tables 3.5 (p.172): Toilet facility; 3.12 (p.179): Households with electricity connection; 4.6 (p.191): Literacy rate] strongly points to this phenomenon. Corroborative evidence comes from southern Africa where Khoisan groups (except in Bushmanland in Namibia) do not wield power in compact territorial settlements, recognised constitutionally, and have a long way to go in the development race. May we suggest that the empowerment of the community concerned is a *sine qua non* for its development, despite the many problems the process of empowerment may be associated with, especially during the initial years of self-determination.

Endnotes

1. Masqueraded as a tribal policy, *Panchsheel* (literally 'five principles'), consists of five broad propositions set out by Jawaharlal Nehru, then Prime Minister of India, in the Foreword he wrote to Verrier Elwin's book *A Philosophy for NEFA* (2nd edition, 1959). There is no evidence that the idea ever received the seal of parliamentary approval or was accepted by the cabinet as the official pronouncement on tribal administration.
2. In 1652, the first European (Dutch) settlement was set up in South Africa at the Cape peninsula initiating European rule. The year 1994 saw the emergence of a democratic South Africa elected by universal franchise
3. The Human Development Index (HDI) was constructed by the United Nations Development Programme to measure human development of different countries of the world. It consists of three indicators, viz. per capita GNP on purchasing parity terms, life expectancy at birth, and literacy rate.
4. These States, in alphabetical order, are (1) Arunachal Pradesh, (2) Chattisgarh, (3) Jharkhand, (4) Manipur, (5) Meghalaya, (6) Mizoram, (7) Nagaland, and (8) Sikkim.
5. Extending the idea of separation to settlement and habitat, the Nationalist Government of South Africa created 'homelands' for different tribal groups. There were ten such homelands, popularly known as Bantustans. Each homeland is supposed to have been the home of a specific tribal group such as the Tswana, the Venda, the Xhosa, the Zulu, etc. Homelands were given limited powers over local administration, but were encouraged to ask for 'independence'. Four of them, viz. Bophuthatswana, Ciskei, Transkei and Venda, did so, but apart from South Africa, no other country recognised their independence. The homelands were re-integrated into the Republic of South Africa, after the demolition of the apartheid system.
6. The languages recognised by the constitution of South Africa as official languages, in alphabetical order, are (1) Afrikaans, (2) English, (3) Ndebele, (4) Pedi, (5) Sotho, (6) Swati, (7) Tsonga, (8) Tswana, (9) Venda, (10) Xhosa, and (11) Zulu.
7. The motto of the Coat of Arms, */Ke e:/xarra//ke*, is a saying of the /Xam people. It means 'Diverse people unite!' Above the motto is a shield containing pictures of two Khoisan people representing the earliest

inhabitants of South Africa. These figures are taken from the Linton Stone, one of the most famous specimens of Khoisan rock art.

8. The term 'creamy layer' refers to the upper crust of the category, 'Other Backward Classes', who are not supposed to benefit from the special privileges extended to the Other Backward Classes.
9. In 1979, the Government of India appointed, under Article 340 of the Constitution, the Second Backward Classes Commission, popularly known as the Mandal Commission (named after its chairman, Justice B.P. Mandal). The Commission was asked to suggest ways and means for giving effect to the objectives of Articles 15 and 16 of the Indian constitution for the prohibition of discrimination and promotion of equality of opportunity in matters of public employment. It was when the Commission's recommendations were being debated in public that a fierce controversy raged over the whole issue of reservation.
10. Currently the numbers of these peoples are estimated to be – Great Andamanese 19; Jarwa 266; and Ongi 108. The population of the Sentinelese is not known, because they live outside the pale of the formal administrative infrastructure. Figures given by Madhusri Mukherji, author of *The Land of Naked People* at a seminar held in Calcutta on 7-8 April, 2004. Report of the Seminar 'Centre has not implemented the directive of the Calcutta High Court and the Supreme Court' (in Bengali), *Anandabazar Patrika* (Bengali daily published from Calcutta), 10 April, 2004.

References

Basu, Durga Das (1998), *Constitutional Law of India.* New Delhi: Prentice-Hall. 7th ed.

Béteille, André (1994) *The Backward Classes in Contemporary India.* Delhi: Oxford University Press.

Bhattacharya, Ashutosh & Rebati Mohan Sarkar (1409 Bengali era/2002 A.D.?) Supplement on Harry Verrier Holman Elwin, *Lok Sanskriti Gabeshana*, Vol.15, No.4 (In Bengali)

Bhattacharya, Satchidananda (1997) *A Dictionary of Indian History.* Calcutta: University of Calcutta.

Jaume, Damia & six colleagues (1993?) 'Racism, Archaeology and Museums: the Strange Case of the Stuffed African Male in the Darder Museum, Banyoles (Catalonia), Spain', *World Archaeological Bulletin* no.6 (1993?)

Dutta, Debasis (1997) *Politics of Reservation Policy in India.* Calcutta: Progressive Publishers.

Elwin, Verrier (1959) *A Philosophy for NEFA*. Shillong: North-East Frontier Agency.

Garrett, John (originally published in 1871 by Higginbotham & Co. Madras; later edition in 1986) *A Classical Dictionary of India*. New Delhi: Oriental Books.

Ghosh, Subodh (1355 Bengali era/1948 A.D.) *Bharater Adibasi*. Kolkata: Indian Associated Publishing Co. (In Bengali)

Government of India: Ministry of Information & Broadcasting, *India 1998: a Reference Manual*. New Delhi

Hardbattle, John Katé (1993) 'Statement on behalf of the First People of Kalahari' in Veber, Hanne; Dahl, Jens; Wilson, Fiona; & Wæhle, Espen (1993) *"...Never Drink from the Same Cup" – Proceedings of the Conference on Indigenous Peoples in Africa, Tune, Denmark, 1993*. Copenhagen: International Work Group for Indigenous Affairs (IWGIA)

Majumdar, D.N. & Madan, T.N. (1957) *An Introduction to Social Anthropology*. Bombay: Asia Publishing House. Ch.16: 'Tribal India: Past, Present and Future'.

Mandelbaum, David G. (original edition published in 1970 by the University of California Press; first Indian edition in 1972; 1998 reprint) *Society in India*. Bombay: Popular Prakashan.

Mogwe, Alice (1992) *Who Was (T) Here First? An Assessment of the Human Rights Situation of Basarwa in Selected Communities in the Gantsi District, Botswana*. Gaborone: Botswana Christian Council.

Muthuswami and Brinda (1998) *Swamy's Compilation on Reservations and Concessions*. Chennai: Swamy Publishers.

Planning Commission, Government of India (2002) *National Human Development Report 2001*. Oxford.

Sanders, A.J.G.M. (1995) *Speaking for the Bushmen*. Gaborone: Botswana Society.

Singh, K.S. (ed.) (1989) *Jawaharlal Nehru, Tribes and Tribal Policy - A Centennial Tribute: Proceedings of a Seminar*. Calcutta: Anthropological Survey of India.

Singh, K.S. (ed.) (1991) *The History of the Anthropological Survey of India: Proceedings of a Seminar*. Calcutta: Anthropological Survey of India.

Singh, K.S. & Datta, Birendranath (eds.) (1993) *Rama-Katha in Tribal and Folk Traditions of India: Proceedings of a Seminar*. Calcutta: Anthropological Survey of India.

Singh, Yogendra (1977; 2nd revised ed. 1997) *Social Stratification and Social Change*. Delhi: Manohar.

Skotness, Pippa (1996) "An Obsession for Khoisan Genitalia" in *Mai! and Guardian*, February 16-22, 1996

Government Communication and Information System (GCIS) (2002) *South African Yearbook 2002/03*. Pretoria: GCIS.

White, Hylton (1995) *In the Tradition of the Forefathers: Bushman Traditionality at Kagga Kamma – The Politics and History of a Performative Identity*. Rondebosch: University of Cape Town, Centre for African Studies.

Index